J. D. Atlas
54 Einstein Drive
Princeton, New Jersey 08540 U.S.A.

Thought and Knowledge

Thought and Knowledge

Essays by

NORMAN MALCOLM

Cornell University Press

ITHACA AND LONDON

First published 1977 by Cornell University Press.
Published in the United Kingdom by Cornell University Press Ltd., 2-4 Brook Street, London W1Y 1AA.

International Standard Book Number 0-8014-1074-6
Library of Congress Catalog Card Number 76-25647
Printed in the United States of America by Vail-Ballou Press, Inc.
Librarians: Library of Congress cataloging information appears on the last page of the book.

TO

Elizabeth Anscombe
Rush Rhees
Georg Henrik von Wright

Contents

Preface

These nine essays, written between 1964 and 1976, are in the philosophy of mind, an area of thought freshly burgeoning with puzzlement and argument. The resurgence of inquiry into the relationship of mind and body has naturally aroused new interest in Descartes' philosophy, and three of the essays are studies of Descartes. In the first I put forward a conjecture as to how he might have supposed himself to have demonstrated that his essential nature is thinking, a conjecture which I do not claim to be verifiable from texts but which, I try to show, has considerable plausibility. In the second I take up Descartes' notorious doctrine that animals, other than men, are automatons without consciousness, and I connect this doctrine with currently favored views about the nature of thinking and thought. In the third I draw attention to a valid deductive argument, considered by Descartes to be a proof that "this I" is a non-material thing, and I display here a confrontation between Descartes' conceptions and those of Wittgenstein.

The fourth essay is a critique of logical behaviorism, with particular reference to the Vienna Circle, B. F. Skinner, and Wittgenstein. The fifth deals with the confusing notion of "the privacy of experience" and attempts to expound some of Wittgenstein's thinking on this difficult topic. The sixth tries to provide an overview of Wittgenstein's treatment of psychological concepts; it includes criticism of William James and the Würzburg psychologists on the nature of thought, and of Wolfgang Köhler's explanation of judgments of "successive comparison." The seventh is a brief thrust at currently influential cognitive psychology, with particular reference to views of Noam Chomsky and Eric Lenneberg on language and thought.

In the eighth essay I return once again to Moore's renowned "defence of common sense," providing a more comprehensive interpretation of it than I have given in my previous essays on this topic. Here I draw on some of the insights contained in Wittgenstein's final writing, *On Certainty*. The ninth essay also relies heavily on this work, trying to relate it to the topic of religious belief.

I am grateful to the following editors, journals, and publishers for permission to republish eight of these essays: to the Editor of *The Philosophical Review* for "Descartes' Proof that His Essence Is Thinking" (*Philosophical Review*, 74, 1965: unrevised); to the American Philosophical Association for "Thoughtless Brutes" (*Proceedings of the American Philosophical Association*, 46, 1972–1973: slightly revised); to the Editor of *Philosophy Forum* and Gordon and Breach, Science Publishers, for permission to use in "Descartes' Proof that He Is Essentially a Non-Material Thing" some observations that appeared in an author/reviewer symposium (*Philosophy Forum*, 14, 1975); to William Marsh Rice University and The University of Chicago Press for "Behaviorism as a Philosophy of Psychology" (*Behaviorism and Phenomenology: Contrasting Bases for Modern Psychology*, ed. T. W. Wann, The University of Chicago Press, Chicago, 1964; copyright © 1964 by William Marsh Rice University: revised); to Avrum Stroll and Harper & Row for "The Privacy of Experience" (*Epistemology: New Essays in the Theory of Knowledge*, ed. Avrum Stroll, Harper & Row, New York, 1967; copyright © 1967 by Avrum Stroll: unrevised); to Nicholas Rescher and the *American Philosophical Quarterly* for "Wittgenstein on the Nature of Mind" (*American Philosophical Quarterly*, Monograph Series, ed. Nicholas Rescher, Monograph No. 4, Oxford, 1970: unrevised); to Theodore Mischel and Academic Press for "The Myth of Cognitive Processes and Structures" (*Cognitive Development and Epistemology*, ed. Theodore Mischel, Academic Press, New York, 1971: unrevised); to Jaakko Hintikka and the Philosophical Society of Finland for "Moore and Wittgenstein on the Sense of 'I know' " (*Essays on Wittgenstein in Honour of G. H. von Wright*, ed. Jaakko Hintikka, *Acta Philosophica Fennica*, 28, 1976: slightly revised); to Stuart Brown, the Royal Institute of Philosophy, and Cornell University Press for "The Groundlessness of Belief" (*Reason and Religion*, ed. Stuart Brown, Royal Institute of Philosophy Conference, 1975, Cornell University Press, Ithaca, forthcoming: revised).

The preparation of this book was accomplished in the spring of 1976, while I was on sabbatic leave from Cornell and while I held a fellowship conferred by the National Endowment for the Humanities. I express my gratitude both to Cornell University and to the National Endowment.

NORMAN MALCOLM

Ithaca, New York

Thought and Knowledge

1 | Descartes' Proof that His Essence Is Thinking

1. SUM RES COGITANS. It is not difficult to understand Descartes' conviction that by means of his "first principle," *cogito ergo sum,* he had proved his own existence with certainty. It is more difficult to understand how he moves from the thesis that, since he thinks, therefore his existence is certain, to the thesis that his nature is nothing but thinking and that he is entirely distinct from his body.[1] His critic, Hobbes, regarded the transition from *cogito ergo sum* to *sum res cogitans* as obviously fallacious: it was like saying, "I am walking, *hence* I am the walking."[2] Another contemporary, Arnauld, was unable to find in the *Meditations* anything like a sound proof of the doctrine *sum res cogitans.*[3] Locke addressed himself to the Cartesian view that "actual thinking is as inseparable from the soul as actual extension is from the body."[4] He saw no support for it save an arbitrary stipulation: "it is but defining the soul to be 'a substance that always thinks,' and the business is done."[5] Locke

---

1. *Oeuvres de Descartes,* ed. C. Adam and P. Tannery (Paris, 1897–1913), VII, 78; *The Philosophical Works of Descartes,* ed. and trans. E. Haldane and G. Ross (Cambridge, 1931), I, 190. The edition of Adam and Tannery is hereafter cited as AT, and that of Haldane and Ross as HR. I use the translations of the latter with occasional changes.
2. *"Sum ambulans, ergo sum ambulatio"* (AT VII, 172; HR II, 61).
3. See AT VII, 197–204; HR II, 80–85.
4. John Locke, *An Essay Concerning Human Understanding,* ed. A. C. Fraser (Oxford, 1894), Bk. II, Ch. i, Sec. 9.
5. Ibid., Sec. 19.

added this tart comment: "If such definition be of any authority, I know not what it can serve for but to make many men suspect that they have no souls at all; since they find a good part of their lives pass away without thinking." [6]

It is not true that the business was done by a mere stipulation. Descartes supported the doctrine *sum res cogitans* with proofs. But it is true that his explicit arguments do not have the force or plausibility that one would expect of the supports of a doctrine so central to his system. To many students of Descartes, the *cogito* is both compelling and profound, but the subsequent demonstrations in his system, supposedly built on the *cogito,* are unconvincing. [7]

I will propose that Descartes' doctrine that his essential nature is thinking is based on a line of thought, not explicitly stated but suggested in various passages, which does have an impressive appearance of cogency. If we attribute this line of thought to Descartes we shall find it easily intelligible that the lucid philosopher should have drawn the conclusion that he was "a substance the whole essence or nature of which is to think." [8] I am interested in Descartes for his own sake; but also I want to understand better what it is that makes his dualism of mind and body a persuasive doctrine, despite the unsatisfactory character of his explicit proofs of it.

2. *Discovering what I am.* Having made certain *that* he is, Descartes undertakes to find out *what* he is. "I know that I exist, and I inquire what I am, I whom I know to exist." [9] He says that he will examine himself attentively. [10] "I must be careful to see that I do not imprudently take *some other object* in place of myself." [11] Descartes is trying to pick out, from various candidates, that which he is. He is searching for that which "pertains" to him or "cannot be

6. Ibid.
7. Speaking of Descartes and the *cogito,* Jaspers says: *"Er kann von dieser Gewissheit aus keinen weiteren Schritt zu neuer Gewissheit tun, der den gleichen Character zwingender Evidenz hätte."* Karl Jaspers, *Descartes und die Philosophie* (2d ed.; Berlin, 1948), p. 18.
8. AT VI, 33; HR I, 101.   9. AT VII, 27; HR I, 152.
10. AT VI, 32 (*examinant avec attention ce que j'étais*); HR I, 101.
11. AT VII, 25; HR I, 150; italics added.

separated" from him.[12] In the language of the *Principles*, he is try-ing to discern his "principal attribute" or "principal property."[13] Or, as Descartes also puts it, he is trying to discover his "essence" or "nature."

Descartes does not explicitly define the terms "essence" or "na-ture." He does say that "nothing without which a thing can still exist is comprised in its essence."[14] The essence of a thing, he is saying, contains only what is necessary for the existence of the thing. Does the essence of a thing contain *everything* that is neces-sary for the existence of the thing? Descartes does not say. But one would think so, for otherwise the essence of a thing would fail to contain something that was essential to that thing—which seems like a contradiction in terms. If the essence of a thing contains *all* that is necessary for the existence of that thing, does it follow that the essence of a thing is *sufficient* (as well as necessary) for the exis-tence of that thing? Apparently not. For if it were so, then the es-sence of anything would imply the existence of that thing; but ac-cording to Descartes, this is true only of the essence of God.[15]

12. AT VII, 26–27; HR I, 151.

13. "Each substance has a principal attribute" (AT VIII, 25; HR I, 240). It is often said that Descartes uncritically assumed that the "I" in "I think" stands for a *substance*. He defined a substance as "a thing which so exists that it needs no other thing in order to exist" (AT VIII, 24; HR I, 239). If he can prove that his essence is solely thinking, and that his existence requires "no world nor place," it would ap-pear to follow that he "needs no other thing in order to exist," i.e., he is a substance. Certainly we should not attribute to Descartes an unreflective assumption on this point.

14. AT VII, 219; HR II, 97.

15. AT VII, 68; HR I, 182. AT VIII, 10; HR, I, 225. Gilson says that, for Des-cartes, the essence of a thing constitutes the thing in itself; the essence of a thing is inseparable from the thing: E. Gilson, *Discours de la Methode: Texte et Commentaire* (Paris, 1947), p. 305. There is a problem here. Descartes certainly would hold that you and I have the same essence, namely, thinking. You can prove that your essence is thinking just as readily as I can prove that my essence is thinking. But from the fact that thinking exists it does not follow that you exist, any more than it follows from the fact that I exist. In this obvious sense, thinking is separable from you and also from me. The essence of a thing, therefore, is separable from the thing; or else thinking is not our essence.

I mention this problem only to leave it. Descartes does not discuss the question of

3. *A criterion for determining my essence.* It is helpful to think of Descartes' procedure in terms of an analogy with sense perception. He has discovered an object, himself; and now he is studying himself attentively in order to make out what his nature is. Descartes states explicitly, of course, that this investigation of himself is not sense perception: "I shall call away all my senses." [16] What I value in the analogy is the picture of a man studying an object in order to make out what it is: "considering my own nature, I shall try little by little to reach a better knowledge of and a more familiar acquaintanceship with myself." [17]

Although Descartes would deny that the essence of a thing is sufficient for the existence of the thing (except in the case of God), he could hold that if there is an existing thing O, and if there is something E, such that if one perceives E, necessarily one perceives O and if one perceives O, necessarily one perceives E, then E is the essence of O. With regard to the existing thing, *himself*, Descartes could hold that if there is something x, such that if he perceives x necessarily he perceives himself and if he perceives himself necessarily he perceives x, then x is his essence. My hypothesis will be that Descartes did hold this view. This hypothesis will suggest a route that could have taken him from the *cogito* to the doctrine *sum res cogitans*.

For my purpose it is not necessary to fasten exclusively on the verb "perceive." Some other verbs of cognition, such as "be aware of" or "apprehend," can be substituted for "perceive." We must constantly remind ourselves of Descartes' frame of thought. He has proved with certainty that he himself exists. He is now going to make *himself* or *his existence* the object of his attention and study. In a striking passage Descartes says that in the *cogito* one's own exis-

---

how there can be numerically different selves with the same essence. This cannot be provided for, on his view, by a difference in bodies or by different locations in space. He did not try to set forth any criteria for the identity and difference of selves, and it is problematic whether he could have done it.

16. AT VII, 34; HR I, 157.   17. Ibid.

tence is something known *per se:* one sees it by a simple act of the mind.[18] He will hold himself (or his existence) before his mental vision. As he observes himself, he will be aware of something which will be what he is, what he consists of, what he can be defined to be.

My suggestion is that Descartes employed the following principle as a criterion for determining his essential nature:

G.   *x* is my essence if it is the case that if I am aware of *x* then (necessarily) I am aware of myself, and if I am aware of myself then (necessarily) I am aware of *x*.[19]

In speaking of the perception, awareness, or knowledge that arises out of the *cogito*, Descartes sometimes calls it a knowledge of *himself*,[20] sometimes a knowledge of *his existence*,[21] and more frequently a knowledge, perception, or awareness *that he exists*. I shall take the liberty of treating the phrases "aware of myself," "aware of my existence," and "aware that I exist," as equivalent in principle G.

4.   *If I am aware of thinking I am aware of myself.* Let us consider whether *thinking* fulfills the first condition contained in principle G. Is it true that if I am aware of thinking then necessarily I am aware of myself or aware that I exist? It should be remembered that Descartes uses the verbs *cogitare* and *penser* in a far wider sense than

18. AT VII, 140; HR II, 38. French version: *"Lorsque quelqu'un dit:* je pense, donc je suis, *ou* j'existe, *il ne conclut pas son existence de sa pensée comme par la force de quelque syllogisme, mais comme une chose connue de soi: il la voit par une simple inspection de l'esprit"* (AT IX, 110).

19. A restriction must be placed on the scope of the variable *x* in this formula, to prevent a silly result. If the value *myself* were substituted for *x*, the result would be that my essence is myself. The term "essence" is not used that way. The value substituted for *x* should be something of which I could be said to "consist": I cannot be said to consist of myself. Without trying to specify further what this requirement might mean, we can at least take the precaution of stipulating that *x* cannot take *myself* as a value.

20. AT VII, 28; HR I, 152. French version: *"cette connaissance que j'ai de moi-même"* (AT IX, 22).

21. See note 18 above.

that in which the English verb "think" is used.[22] To feel or to seem to oneself to feel any sensation (for example, to seem to feel heat),[23] to doubt, to deny, to imagine, to will, to be actively aware of anything, would be "to think," in Descartes' broad use of *cogitare*. It should also be noted that Descartes holds that we are aware of every thought we have: "*Thought* is a word that covers everything that exists in us in such a way that we are immediately conscious of it." [24] As a result of these two points it is true that, for Descartes, if I am aware of anything then I am thinking, and so if I am aware of thinking then I am thinking; and if I am thinking I am aware of thinking.

Does Descartes hold that whenever I think I am aware of myself (or aware that I exist)? If he does, then he is committed to holding that I am aware of myself at every moment: for he holds that I am

22. Some commentators claim that this wide usage was common in the everyday French of the seventeenth century and in medieval Latin. (See A. Koyré's introduction to *Descartes' Philosophical Writings*, ed. E. Anscombe and P. Geach [Edinburgh, 1954], p. xxxvii; cf. the Translators' Note, p. xlvii). Whether or not this is so, I can see a purely philosophical basis for Descartes' broad use of *cogitare* and *penser*. Descartes says: "Of my thoughts some are, so to speak, images of the things, and to these alone is the title 'idea' properly applied; examples are my thought of a man or of a chimera, of heaven, of an angel, or of God. But other thoughts possess other forms as well. For example in willing, fearing, approving, denying, though I always perceive (*apprehendo*) something *as the object of my thought* (*ut subjectum meae cogitationis*), yet by this action I always add something else to the idea which I have of that thing; and of the thoughts of this kind some are called volitions or affections, and other judgments" (AT VII, 37; HR I, 159; italics added). In logic and grammar *subjectum* means "that which is spoken of." It seems fair to translate *subjectum meae cogitationis* as "the object of my thought." What Descartes holds is that if I am imagining, or willing, or sensing, or feeling, etc., there is always an object before my mind, an object of direct awareness. If I *approve* of something, for example, there is an object of awareness, plus some further "attitude." The same holds for all other mental events. What is common to all of them is that there is an object of awareness. It is natural to call that state of affairs in which something is directly before the mind as an object, *thought*, or *thinking*. Thus it is intelligible and plausible that Descartes should have regarded all forms of consciousness as species of *thinking*, regardless of the contemporary popular and philosophical usage of *penser* and *cogitare*.

23. AT VII, 29; HR I, 153.   24. AT VII, 160; HR II, 52.

thinking at every moment.[25] Surely it is unlikely, one will think, that Descartes would have believed that at every moment of my life I have the actual thought *I exist*. But metaphysical philosophy does not obtain its inspiration from common sense. Let us consider whether there is any evidence that Descartes did hold that every moment of my life I am aware of myself (or of my existence, or that I exist).

The evidence from his writings is not decisive. In *The Search After Truth* Polyander says: "If I did not think, I could not know whether I doubt or exist. Yet I am, and know that I am, and I know it because I doubt, that is to say because I think. And better, it might be that if I ceased for an instant to think I should cease at the same time to be." [26] These remarks could be taken as suggesting the view that to know that one exists it is sufficient to think. In the *Second Meditation* Descartes says: "I am, I exist, that is certain. But how long? As long as I think; for it might possibly be the case that if I ceased entirely to think, I should likewise cease altogether to exist." [27] Here Descartes might be saying that as long as he thinks, and only when he thinks, it is certain that he exists. But the passage is difficult. In *Discourse IV* he says: "I saw from the very fact that I thought of doubting the truth of other things, it very evidently and certainly followed that I was; on the other hand, if I had only ceased from thinking, even if all the rest of what I had ever imagined had really existed, I should have no reason for thinking that I had existed." [28] When he is not thinking, he "has no reason for thinking" he exists. What this suggests is that whenever he is thinking, he does have a "reason for thinking" he exists. But still, one does not actually think at every moment of all the reasons

25. Letter to Gibieuf, 19 January 1642 (AT III, 478).

26. AT X, 521; HR I, 322.

27. AT VII, 27; HR I, 151–152. I follow Hintikka in reading *Quandiu autem?* as "But how long?" and *Nempe quandiu* as "As long as" (Jaakko Hintikka, *"Cogito, Ergo Sum:* Inference or Performance?," *Philosophical Review,* 71 [1962], 22).

28. AT VI, 32–33; HR I, 101. For further evidence on the point at issue see note 60 below.

one has for believing various things; so this remark need not imply that one is always thinking of a reason for thinking one exists.

Descartes' own statements admittedly do not provide strong evidence for his having held that whenever I think I am aware that I exist. I believe it is plausible, however, that he would be drawn to accept this doctrine. This is partly because the best support for his principle "I think, *ergo* I exist" is at the same time a support for the principle "I think, *ergo* I am aware that I exist." I shall explain this later (Sections 14–16) and shall assume for the present that Descartes would admit that whenever I am thinking I am aware that I exist.

Assuming this to be so, thinking fulfills the first condition of principle *G*, namely, if I am aware of thinking I am aware of myself. For Descartes would agree that if I am aware of thinking then I am thinking, and (by our assumption) that if I am thinking I am aware of myself. It follows that if I am aware of thinking I am aware of myself.

5. *If I am aware of myself, I am aware of thinking.* It is easy to see that the second condition of principle *G* holds for *thinking*. According to Descartes, we are aware of every thought we have. Being aware of myself would be a particular example of thinking. Therefore, if I am aware of myself I am aware of thinking.

6. *Thinking is my essence.* Thinking satisfies the two conditions of principle *G* and is therefore proved to be my essence. The reasoning by which this result is achieved would be very natural for Descartes, and also it appears to be rigorous.

To recapitulate: Descartes' first step in rebuilding the structure of human knowledge is to prove that a particular thing exists, namely, himself. Next he seeks to find out the nature of this thing. He proceeds to deduce by highly intuitive principles and with every appearance of cogency that what constitutes the nature of this thing (himself) is thinking. For he is aware of himself if and only if he is aware of thinking.

This method of proving the doctrine *sum res cogitans* was not explicitly formulated by Descartes, and so my attribution of it to him is necessarily a conjecture. But if we assume that this line of thought lay unclearly in his mind, it becomes easier to understand the passage in the *Discourse* where he first announces his discovery of the separateness of mind and body:

And then, examining attentively that which I was, I saw that I could conceive that I had no body, and that there was no world nor place where I might be; but yet that I could not for all that conceive that I was not. On the contrary, I saw from the very fact that I thought of doubting the truth of other things, it very evidently and certainly followed that I was; on the other hand if I had only ceased from thinking, even if all the rest of what I had ever imagined had really existed, I should have no reason for thinking that I had existed. *From that I knew that I was a substance the whole essence or nature of which is to think,* and that for its existence there is no need of any place, nor does it depend on any material thing: so that this "me," that is to say, the soul by which I am what I am, is entirely distinct from body, and is even more easy to know than is the latter; and even if body were not, the soul would not cease to be what it is.[29]

The line of thought that I am attributing to Descartes would also help to make intelligible the otherwise puzzling passage in *Meditation VI:* "Just because I know certainly that I exist, and that meanwhile I do not notice (*animadvertam*) that any other thing necessarily pertains to my nature or essence, excepting that I am a thinking thing, I rightly conclude that my essence consists solely in the fact that I am a thinking thing." [30]

It is evident that *body* or *my body* cannot satisfy both conditions of principle *G*. To be sure, if I am aware of my body (or indeed of anything) then, according to Descartes, I am aware of myself. But it is false that if I am aware of myself then necessarily I am aware of my body. It is not difficult to imagine cases in which a man is not aware of his body (suppose he has lost all sensory power and feeling): yet he can still think to himself *"Ego sum, ego existo."* Descartes can be aware of himself even if he is not aware of anything

29. Ibid.; italics added.   30. AT VII, 78; HR I, 190.

corporeal. The criterion provided by principle *G* cannot give the result that any corporeal thing is his essence. Since it does give the result that thinking is his essence, and since a substance can have no more than one essence, Descartes is apparently entitled to hold that he is "entirely and absolutely distinct" from his body "and can exist without it." [31]

7. *I do not know that body pertains to my nature,* ergo *it does not.* In the *Preface to the Reader*, which Descartes published with the *Meditations*, he takes note of a criticism that had been made of his previously published *Discourse on Method*. The criticism, he states, is that "it does not follow from the fact that the human mind reflecting on itself does not perceive itself to be other than a thing that thinks, that its nature or its essence consists only in its being a thing that thinks, in the sense that this word *only* excludes all other things which might also be supposed to pertain to the nature of the soul." Descartes goes on to remark: "To this objection I reply that it was not my intention in that place [the *Discourse*] to exclude these in accordance with the order that looks to the truth of the matter (as to which I was not then dealing), but only in accordance with the order of my perception (*perceptionem*): thus my meaning was that so far as I was aware, I knew nothing clearly as belonging to my essence, excepting that I was a thing that thinks, or a thing that has in itself the faculty of thinking. *But I shall show hereafter how from the fact that I know no other thing which pertains to my essence, it follows that there is no other thing which really does belong to it.*" [32]

Descartes gives here a wrong account of his intentions in the *Discourse*. If one examines the passage from the *Discourse* quoted in the preceding section, one sees that Descartes was *not* asserting merely that "so far as I was aware, I knew nothing clearly as belonging to my essence, except that I was a thing that thinks." On the contrary he asserts, categorically and without qualification, "I knew that I

31. Ibid.   32. AT VII, 7–8; HR I, 137–138; italics added.

was a substance the whole essence or nature of which is to think." [33]

But for my purpose the chief interest of the passage from the *Preface* is to show that Descartes does maintain that from the fact that he *knows* of nothing other than thinking that pertains to his essence, it follows that nothing else does pertain to it.

Arnauld acutely criticized Descartes' proof, in the *Meditations*, that his nature was solely thinking. Arnauld's main point is that one may not *know* that y is essential to x, and yet it may be true that y is essential to x. By reasoning that is parallel to Descartes', says Arnauld, a man would be entitled to argue as follows: "While I clearly and distinctly perceive that this triangle is right-angled, I yet doubt whether the square on its base is equal to the squares on its sides. Hence the equality of the square on the base to those on the sides does not belong to its essence." [34] How can it follow, asks Arnauld, "from the fact that one is unaware that anything else belongs to one's essence, except that one is a thinking being, that nothing else really belongs to one's essence?" [35]

If one understands Descartes' "argument from ignorance," as one might want to call it, in the way that Descartes himself states it in the *Preface* [36] and in the way that Arnauld restates it, then it is obviously fallacious. From the fact that one does not *know* of anything other than y that is essential to x, it does not follow that nothing else is essential.

If, however, we conceive of Descartes as reasoning in accordance with principle G, as previously described, then his proof is no longer obviously fallacious. On the contrary it seems flawless. And also it no longer appears to be an argument from *ignorance*. We can understand why Descartes, who sought to introduce the rigor of mathematics into metaphysics, and who believed that he had "very exact demonstrations" [37] of everything in the *Meditations*, was so

33. AT VI, 33; HR I, 101.   34. AT VII, 201–202; HR II, 83.
35. AT VII, 199; HR II, 81.   36. AT VII, 8; HR I, 138.
37. AT VII, 13, HR I, 140.

confident that he had discovered his essential nature. In replying to Arnauld he says, "Although perhaps there is much in me of which I have no knowledge . . . *yet since that which I am aware of in myself is sufficient to allow of my existing with it as my sole possession,* I am certain that God could have created me without giving me those other things of which I am not yet aware." [38] Descartes was sure that he could exist with thinking as his sole possession, because his perception of thinking was seen by him to be both a necessary and sufficient condition of his perception of himself.

8.   *I have a clear and distinct idea of mind apart from body.* Descartes remarks in several places that it is not proved until the *Sixth Meditation* that mind is distinct from body. [39] The proof occurring in this *Meditation* is that since he has a clear and distinct idea of himself "as only a thinking and unextended thing" (*quatenus sum tantum res cogitans, non extensa*), [40] God's omnipotence could make him exist apart from body, and therefore he is distinct from body.

It is necessary to ask what assures Descartes that he has a clear and distinct idea (conception, perception) of himself as an unextended thing. If this is merely a dogmatic assertion, then the proof from clear and distinct ideas has no value. It would be unlike Descartes and contrary to his aims to be dogmatic on so crucial a point. He needs an objective proof that he has a clear and distinct idea of himself as an unextended thing. On our present interpretation, this first premise of the argument from clear and distinct ideas is established as true by Descartes' demonstrative proof that he is aware of himself when and only when he is aware of thinking. Awareness of body does not come into it. This would seem to be as good a proof as could be demanded that he has *a clear and distinct perception* of himself as solely a thinking thing.

38. AT VII, 219; HR II, 97; italics added.
39. E.g., AT VII, 13; HR I, 140–141. AT VII, 175; HR II, 63. AT VII, 131; HR II, 32.
40. AT VII, 78; HR I, 190. Cf. AT VII, 169–170; HR II, 59.

9. *Why Descartes declares that the separateness of mind from body is not proved until the* Sixth Meditation. In support of the suggestion that Descartes employed the criterion of principle G to determine his essence, I cited evidence from the *Fourth Discourse* and the *Second Meditation*. But since Descartes declares that he has not proved the separateness of mind from body until the *Sixth Meditation*, does not this destroy that evidence and refute my suggestion?

No. What is delayed until the *Sixth Meditation* is the resolution of the radical doubt as to whether our clear and distinct perceptions (ideas, conceptions) may not be mistaken. This is a doubt as to whether there is any correspondence at all between reality and our clear and distinct perceptions. Having proved that there is a God, and that all things depend on Him, and that He is not a deceiver, Descartes deduces, at the end of *Meditation V*, that "what I perceive clearly and distinctly cannot fail to be true." [41] Armed with this conclusion, Descartes can then assert, in *Meditation VI*, that "it suffices that I am able to apprehend one thing apart from another clearly and distinctly in order to be certain that the one is different from the other." [42] Since he has previously determined that he perceives himself clearly and distinctly as "only a thinking and unextended thing," he deduces that in reality he is a distinct thing from his body. [43]

Our interpretation is not concerned with his radical, metaphysical doubt, but only with his assertion that he has a clear and distinct perception of himself as solely a thinking thing. Since this assertion is made both in *Discourse IV* and *Meditation II*, we are warranted in drawing evidence for our interpretation from those texts. [44]

---

41. AT VII, 70; HR I, 184.   42. AT VII, 78; HR I, 190.   43. Ibid.
44. My interpretation disagrees with that of Hamelin, who says of Descartes' position in *Meditation II*, "*S'il dit qu'il est une chose qui pense, cela signifie qu'il n'est autorisé pour le moment à se considérer que comme une chose qui pense.*" O. Hamelin, *Le Système de Descartes* (Paris, 1911), p. 127. We have seen that in *Discourse IV* Descartes asserts, without qualification, that his whole essence is to think (Section 7, above). In *Meditation II* he says: "I do not now admit anything which is not necessarily true: to speak accurately I am only (*tantum*) a thing which thinks" (AT VII, 27; HR I, 152).

10. *The indivisibility of the mind.* In *Meditation VI* Descartes has a supplementary argument for the separateness of mind and body, which would be sufficient, he says, to prove that "the mind or soul of man is entirely different from the body," if he had not already proved it by his argument from clear and distinct ideas.[45] His additional argument is that body is divisible and mind is indivisible. "When I consider the mind, that is to say, myself inasmuch as I am only a thinking thing, I cannot distinguish in myself any parts, but apprehend myself to be clearly one and entire; and although the whole mind seems to be united to the whole body, yet if a foot, or an arm, or some other part, is separated from my body, I am aware that nothing has been taken away from my mind." [46] In the *Synopsis* of the *Meditations* Descartes declares that "we are not able to conceive of the half of a mind as we can do of the smallest of all bodies; so that we see that not only are their natures different but even in some respects contrary to one another." [47]

This supplementary argument is very weak. It is true that thinking is not divisible into spatial parts. But neither is weight: yet it does not follow that weight is not a property of bodies. If Descartes were offering, as an *empirical* consideration, the claim that people who have lost some parts of their bodies have found nothing taken away from their minds, it would be unconvincing. Has someone who lost his head been aware that he suffered no loss of mind?

Descartes is saying that *I* am not divisible into spatial parts. But that is not so. I can be split in half. Descartes would reply that "I" would mean here "my body": when "I" refers only to a thinking

---

The assertion is again unqualified. I suspect that two things, mainly, have prevented Hamelin and other commentators from taking these assertions literally: first, the postponing of the final resolution of the radical, metaphysical doubt until *Meditation VI;* second, a failure to perceive how Descartes could have believed that he had proved, in *Meditation II* and *Discourse IV,* that (leaving aside the metaphysical doubt) his nature is solely thinking. The result is the view that in the *Discourse* and *Meditation II* Descartes did not assert that he really is nothing but a thing which thinks. Descartes' own misinterpretation of the *Discourse* (see Section 7 above) also helps to make this view attractive.

45. AT VII, 86; HR I, 196.   46. Ibid.   47. AT VII, 13; HR I, 141.

and unextended thing, I am not divisible into spatial parts. But does "I" *ever* refer solely to a thinking and unextended thing? Descartes needs to establish that this is so: therefore he has to rely on his proof that I am only a thinking and unextended thing. Thus his "supplementary" argument is not truly a separate argument: it depends on his previous argument that I have a clear and distinct idea of myself as a thinking and unextended thing. This latter argument, we have proposed, relies on the criterion provided by principle *G*.

11. *What I can and cannot doubt.* Descartes employs the technique of doubting everything for which there is any possible ground of doubt in order to try to find something that is certain beyond all possible ground of doubt. He finds that he can doubt that he has a body but not that he exists. On this difference he constructs still another argument for the separateness of mind and body. In the dialogue *The Search After Truth*, Polyander says to Eudoxus: "I know very well that what I am inasmuch as I doubt, is in no wise what I call my body. And more than that, I do not even know that I have a body, since you have shown me that I might doubt of it. . . . Yet, while entirely setting aside all these suppositions, this will not prevent my being certain that I exist. On the contrary, they confirm me yet more in the certainty that I exist and that I am not a body; *otherwise, doubting of my body I should at the same time doubt of myself*, and this I cannot do." [48]

These remarks contain the following argument, briefly put:

> I can doubt that I have a body.
> I cannot doubt that I exist.
> *Ergo*, I am not a body.

The same argument occurs twice in the *Principles*. [49] In the first of these two occurrences the conclusion is "Body does not pertain to

48. AT X, 518; HR I, 319; italics added.
49. Pt. I, Principles 7 and 8, and Principle 60 (AT VIII, 6–7, 29; HR I, 221, 244).

my nature" (instead of "I am not a body"); in the second it is "I am distinct from corporeal substance." In the *Notae in Programma*, the following argument occurs: "I wrote that we could not doubt that our mind existed, because, from the very fact that we doubted, it followed that our mind existed, but that meantime we might doubt whether any material thing existed; whence I deduced and demonstrated that mind was clearly perceived by us as an existence, or substance, even supposing we had no concept whatever of the body, or even denied that any material things had existence; and, accordingly, that the concept of mind does not involve any concept of body." [50] In *Discourse IV* there is a hint of the same argument,[51] but it is conflated with the test for determining one's essential nature that is described in Section 3 above. There is a suggestion of the argument from doubt in the *Synopsis* of the *Meditations*,[52] although there is not much indication of it in the *Meditations*. [53] This argument is also indicated in the *Author's Letter*, which serves as a preface to the *Principles:* "Thus in considering that he who would doubt all things cannot yet doubt that he exists while he doubts, and that what reasons so in being unable to doubt of itself and yet doubting all else, is not what we call our body but what we call our soul or thought." [54]

12. *Criticism of the argument from doubt.* It is sufficiently evident that Descartes argued from the premise that he could doubt the existence of his body but could not doubt his own existence, to the conclusion either that he was not his body, or that there was no essential connection between him and his body. Although the argument is undoubtedly attractive, we can prove that it is invalid by constructing arguments of parallel form that are plainly invalid. I shall not be concerned with the truth of the premises but solely

50. AT VIII, 354, HR I, 440.

51. See the paragraph from the *Discourse* quoted in Section 6 above.

52. AT VII, 12–13; HR I, 140.

53. It is worth noting, however, that Arnauld thought that the argument from doubt does occur in the *Meditations.* See AT VII, 198; HR II, 80.

54. AT IX, 9–10; HR I, 208.

with validity—that is, with whether the conclusion follows from the premises.

It might be true of a man that he could doubt that he is a Grand Master of the Elks but could not doubt that he exists; it would not follow that he is not a Grand Master of the Elks. It might be true that I could not doubt that Bertrand Russell exists but I could doubt that the author of the pamphlet "Why I Am Not a Christian" exists; it would not follow that Bertrand Russell is not the author of that pamphlet.

It might be objected that in these counterexamples the conclusions are contingent propositions, whereas the conclusion of Descartes' argument from doubt was intended to be an a priori proposition—namely, the a priori proposition that there is no necessary connection between me and a body. It might be thought that Descartes' argument could validly prove an a priori conclusion, if not a contingent one. But it is easy to construct an argument of the same form, which has an a priori conclusion, yet is obviously invalid. For example, it might be true that I could not doubt that the number of people in my living room was 17 (because I had counted them carefully) but I could doubt (because I get confused about prime numbers) that the number of people there was equal to the only prime number between 13 and 19. The argument we are constructing will have the following premises:

> I can doubt that the number is equal to the only prime between 13 and 19.
> I cannot doubt that the number is 17.

Following the model of the argument from doubt, the conclusion will be either: there is no essential connection between the number 17 and the number that is equal to the only prime between 13 and 19; or: the number 17 is not the only prime between 13 and 19. Since the conclusion, in either form, is false, whereas the premises could be true, it is shown that the form of argument is invalid. The argument from doubt is not rendered *more* valid by being provided with an a priori conclusion.

Descartes' argument from doubt also makes him vulnerable to an *argumentum ad hominem*. *If* it were valid to argue "I can doubt that my body exists but not that I exist, *ergo* I am not my body," it would be equally valid to argue "I can doubt that there exists a being whose essential nature is to think, but I cannot doubt that I exist, *ergo* I am not a being whose essential nature is to think." Descartes is hoist with his own petard! A form of argument that he employs to help establish the doctrine *sum res cogitans* could be used, if it were valid, to refute that very doctrine.

13. *Criticism of Descartes' criterion.* Let us turn back to study the criterion that Descartes used in his most cogent-seeming proof that thinking was his essential nature. As we said, the idea behind this criterion is that he will examine himself to find out *what* he perceives when he perceives himself. His procedure can be presented as the following deductive argument:

G. x is my essence if it is the case that (a) if I am aware of x then (necessarily) I am aware of myself, and (b) if I am aware of myself then (necessarily) I am aware of x.
Thinking satisfies these conditions.
Ergo, thinking is my essence.

We may think of principle G as being composed of two tests, (a) and (b), each of which is to be used to eliminate candidates for what my essence is, in the sense that any candidate failing to satisfy either (a) or (b) thereby fails to satisfy the criterion of principle G. Test (a) will be thought of in the following way: when I am aware of some candidate, x, I will observe whether I am aware of myself (or aware that I exist). If I am not aware that I exist, then x does not satisfy the criterion.

It is not difficult to see, however, that it would be impossible for me to make the "observation" that I am not aware that I exist. Test (a) cannot serve to eliminate *any* candidates. Therefore it is not a genuine test. It is not really a method for helping to determine my essence.

14. *Self-defeating utterances.* In his brilliant article on Descartes'
cogito,[55] Professor Jaakko Hintikka makes a case for interpreting
Descartes' "I think therefore I exist" as something other than a logical inference from "I think" to "I exist." Hintikka calls our attention to the fact that although the *sentence* "Descartes does not exist"
is formally consistent, it would be absurd for *Descartes* to utter this
sentence in order to persuade an auditor, who knew that the
speaker was Descartes, that Descartes does not exist.[56] This utterance, or statement, would be "self-defeating," as Hintikka puts it.
If now we consider the sentence obtained by substituting the personal pronoun "I" for the proper name "Descartes" (that is, "I do
not exist") we see that the utterance of this sentence by anyone
would always be self-defeating.[57] No speaker could, by saying
those words, convince anyone (including himself) that what he says
is true. Hintikka suggests that the principle "I think therefore I
exist" should be conceived, in part at least, as an expression of Descartes' realization that one's attempt to say or think that oneself
does not exist yields a statement that is necessarily self-defeating.

This is an illuminating interpretation of the *cogito.* Now it can be
seen that if the utterance "I do not exist" is self-defeating, so is the
utterance "I am not *aware* that I exist."

Sometimes a statement of the form "I am not aware that *p*" provides evidence that *p* is false. My statement "I am not *aware* of a
strong odor" could be evidence, for you, that there is no strong
odor. If I say to you in regard to a drawn figure before me, "I am
not aware that one side is shorter than the other," this might give
you a reason for believing that one side is not shorter than the
other. My not being aware of something can be evidence that the
something is not so.

Suppose, however, that someone has the suspicion that I do not
exist. By making the statement "I am not *aware* that I exist" I can-

55. Hintikka, *"Cogito, Ergo Sum:* Inference or Performance?" (See also his *"Cogito,
Ergo Sum* as an Inference and a Performance," *Philosophical Review,* 72 [1963], 487.)
56. Hintikka, *"Cogito, Ergo Sum:* Inference or Performance?", 12–13.
57. Ibid., 14.

not verify his suspicion. Quite the contrary. And if we imagine (absurdly) that *I* am uncertain as to whether *I* exist, my declaration to myself, "I am not *aware* that I exist," would not express anything that could be a reason for me to blieve that I do not exist.

It would seem that the purpose of saying "I am not aware that *p*" is either to persuade someone (possibly oneself) that *p* is false, or to express a doubt (including noncommitment) that *p* is true. Certainly one cannot *assert p* and in the same breath assert that one is not aware that *p;* for example, one cannot assert: "It rained yesterday but I am not aware that it did." In saying "I am not aware that *p*," one's attitude toward *p* must be doubt or denial.

In the special case in which "I exist" is the value for *p*, the purpose for which a statement of the form "I am not aware that *p*" is made cannot be achieved. The statement "I am not aware that I exist" has to imply a denial or a doubt of the speaker's own existence—that is, it has to imply that it is possible to assert or to think "I do not exist" or "Possibly I do not exist." Now since these latter statements would be self-defeating, therefore the statement "I am not aware that I exist" has a second-order, self-defeating character.[58]

I believe that the ultimate logical truth underlying Descartes' *cogito* is the fact that the statement "I do not exist" is necessarily self-defeating. If this is so, then Descartes' most formidable argument for holding that his essence is thinking is derived from the very same foundation that supports the *cogito*.

15. *Further consideration of Descartes' criterion.* We noticed that Descartes' criterion of his essential nature can be divided into two tests. The idea of test (a) is that when I am aware of something, *x*, I should observe whether I am aware that I exist. If I observe that I am not aware that I exist, then *x* does not satisfy the criterion. We saw that the self-defeating nature of this "observation" makes it im-

58. For a study of various types of "self-defeating" or "indefensible" statements, see Hintikka's book, *Knowledge and Belief* (Ithaca, N.Y., 1962).

possible for this test to have a negative result. The test will necessarily be satisfied for every value of "*x*," and so the fact that it is satisfied for the value *thinking* has no tendency to show that *thinking* is my essence.

The second test contained in Descartes' criterion is test (b): "If I am aware that I exist I am aware of *x*." Suppose I wanted to determine whether *breathing* is my essence. *Breathing* will pass test (a), since everything passes it. Let us try test (b). If I am aware that I exist, is it necessarily the case that I am aware of breathing? No. So *breathing* is eliminated. We noted previously (Section 6) that *my body* is eliminated as a candidate by test (b).

We know that *thinking* passes test (b). But why does it? This is easily explained. Awareness of anything whatever is *thinking*, in Descartes' broad use of the term (Section 4). So if I am aware that I exist, then I am thinking. We noted the Cartesian doctrine that if I am thinking I am aware of thinking (ibid.). It follows that if I am aware that I exist I am aware of thinking.

But this analysis reveals that the fact that *thinking* passes test (b) has no tendency to show that it is the essence of *myself*. In the conditional, "If I am aware of myself (aware that I exist) then I am aware of thinking," we can substitute anything whatever into the antecedent, in place of the value *myself*, and always obtain a necessarily true proposition. The particular value *myself* is irrelevant to the truth of the conditional. "If I am aware of breathing then I am aware of thinking" is necessarily true. "If I am aware of an old tire then I am aware of thinking" is necessarily true. And so on. The truth of the condition, "If I am aware of myself I am aware of thinking," does not depend on the value *myself*.

16. *Reviewing Descartes' criterion.* Descartes' criterion for determining that thinking is my essence has the look of being airtight. Thinking is my essence if these two conditions hold: (a) when I am aware of thinking I am aware of myself; (b) when I am aware of myself I am aware of thinking.

Not only is this a plausible criterion but, furthermore, propositions (a) and (b) are both necessarily true. What more cogent proof could there be that my essential nature is thinking?

We are presented with the paradox that, although thinking apparently does satisfy Descartes' criterion, nonetheless it is not established that my nature is thinking! Our analysis of why conditions (a) and (b) are true shows that this is not because of any necessary connection between myself (or my existence) and thinking. Condition (a) is true solely because the statement "I am not aware of myself" is self-defeating: this is what prevents me from making the observation that I am aware of thinking but not aware of myself. The self-defeating character of the statement "I am not aware of myself" is derivative from the self-defeating character of the statement "I do not exist," and so condition (a) has the same basis as does the *cogito*. Condition (b) is true because the awareness of anything is "thinking," and also because of Descartes' doctrine that one cannot think without being aware of thinking.

This doctrine that one cannot think without being aware of thinking could itself be justified by the self-defeating nature of the statement "I am not aware of thinking." The statement "I am not thinking" (in Descartes' broad sense of "thinking") is as self-defeating as "I do not exist." In exactly the same way in which we showed that "I am not aware that I exist" has a second-order, self-defeating character, derived from "I do not exist," we could show that the statement "I am not aware that I am thinking" has a second-order, self-defeating character, derived from "I am not thinking." Thus we can regard the metaphysical thesis *sum res cogitans* as obtaining its *entire* support from the self-defeating nature of the two statements "I am not aware that I exist" and "I am not aware that I think." This may help in understanding why Descartes regarded the *cogito* as being so *fruitful*. For the logical truth that underlies the *cogito*, together with another of exactly the same character, could seem to Descartes to provide an immediate transition from the *cogito* to the important theme that his nature is solely thinking.

We may conceive of Descartes' criterion (principle *G*) as being obtained by substitution on the variables in the formula "x is the essence of y if the awareness of x is logically equivalent to the awareness of y." [59] I am not claiming that this formula is a logical truth, or even that it is very meaningful. Nevertheless it has a high degree of intuitive plausibility. If one's undertaking is to determine the essence of a certain thing (for example, a triangle) and if in the process of studying this thing one hit upon something that satisfied the mentioned formula (for example, a three-sided plane figure) it would be very compelling to believe that the undertaking had been successfully completed.

My criticism is that even if we assume that the formula gives a correct method of determination in *all* other cases, and even though it is a fact that, when *thinking* and *myself* are substituted for x and y, the conditions (a) and (b) thus obtained are necessarily true, it is still not established that *thinking* and *myself* (or *my existence*) are essentially connected.

A statement of the form "When I am aware of x I am aware of myself" is necessarily true regardless of the value for x. The fact that it is true when the value is *thinking* does not reveal any necessary relation between thinking and myself. Also a statement of the form "When I am aware of y I am aware of thinking" is necessarily true regardless of the value for y. The fact that it is true when the value is *myself* does not reveal any necessary relation between myself and thinking. Neither condition of Descartes' criterion shows any essential connection between thinking and myself, although there is every appearance of the criterion's being satisfied.

It would be desirable to make explicit the sense in which the conditionals (a) and (b) of Descartes' criterion are "necessarily true." We can distinguish two senses in which a conditional can be necessarily true. In the first sense, a conditional is necessarily true if the negation of the consequent is inconsistent with the antecedent. Descartes' proof has *not* shown that the conditionals (a) and (b) are necessarily true in this sense. But this is the sense required to

---

59. Remembering that x and y must take different values. Cf. note 19 above.

prove that *thinking* and *myself* are essentially connected. A conditional is necessarily true, in the second sense, if it is self-defeating to deny the consequent. The conditionals (a) and (b) are necessarily true in this sense. The seeming cogency of the proof employing the criterion of principle *G* may derive from a confusing of these two senses of "necessarily true."

It is worth noting that the conditional "If I think, I exist" (which might be taken as a version of the *cogito*) is necessarily true in *both* senses. Hintikka's studies provide good evidence that Descartes did not clearly distinguish these two aspects of the *cogito*. Previously (Section 4) I asked whether it was credible that Descartes should have supposed that whenever I am thinking I am aware that I exist, in the sense of having the actual thought *I exist*. I think it is credible. For the conditional "If I think, I exist" is necessarily true in two ways that Descartes did not disentangle. The conditional "If I think, I am aware that I exist" is necessarily true in only one of those ways. It is not implausible that Descartes should have made the half-conscious assumption that this second conditional, being necessarily true, has the feature (possessed by the first one) that the consequent *follows from* the antecedent. He would thus be led to believe (mistakenly) that since it is true that I exist at every moment I am thinking, so it is true that I am aware that I exist at every moment I am thinking.[60]

---

60. Descartes wrote to Mersenne, in July 1641, that *"il est impossible que nous puissons jamais penser à aucune chose, que nous n'avons en même temps l'idée de notre Ame"* (AT III, 394). Is Descartes affirming here the view that whenever I think of anything I am aware of myself, i.e., aware that I exist? What he says is that it is impossible for me to think of anything unless I have the *idea* of myself (of my soul). This could mean merely that it is a necessary condition of my doing any thinking that I should have the *concept* of myself. It would not have to mean that whenever I think I have an actual thought of myself. Yet if this is what Descartes meant, then why should he say that I cannot think of anything unless *at the same time* I have the idea of my soul? This temporal specification makes it appear that he is talking about having an actual thought, rather than about having a concept.

SUMMARY

Descartes actually states three proofs of the thesis that I am only a thinking and unextended thing. One is the argument from doubt: I can doubt that my body exists but not that I exist; therefore my body does not pertain to my essential nature. This argument is invalid. Another proof is the argument from clear and distinct ideas: I have a clear and distinct idea of myself as a thinking and unextended thing and of body as an extended and unthinking thing; therefore I am separate and distinct from body. This argument requires support for the premise that I have a clear and distinct idea of myself as a thinking and unextended thing. The third proof is the argument from the indivisibility of myself: *I* am indivisible but my body is divisible; therefore my body does not pertain to my essence. This argument requires support for the premise that *I* am indivisible.

Descartes has another argument that is never set down in so many words, but is suggested by various passages. This argument appears to provide a complete demonstration of the doctrine *sum res cogitans*, and also to give the needed support to the second and third arguments. This new argument has an appearance of extreme rigor and cogency, although it is actually invalid. Attributing this argument to Descartes helps to explain why he thought he could make the transition from *cogito ergo sum* to *sum res cogitans:* for the seeming solidity and power of this argument is mainly derived from the *cogito* itself.

2 | Thoughtless Brutes

I

When readers of Descartes first come upon his theme that animals are automatons, lacking consciousness, they are astonished. As Zeno Vendler says in his recent book, *Res Cogitans*, "the notorious doctrine of the automatism of brutes" is "perhaps the most counterintuitive item" in Descartes' philosophy.[1] Descartes himself had no concern for the "counterintuitive" character of his thesis. He declares that the belief that animals "act by an interior principle like the one within ourselves, that is to say, by means of a soul which has feeling and passions like ours," is an outstanding example of prejudice. One cannot, he says, present the reasons against this belief "without exposing oneself to the ridicule of children and feeble minds."[2]

The doctrine of the automatism of animals was a topic of much controversy for a century and a half after Descartes' death. It was even claimed by some opponents of the doctrine that the Cartesians were deliberately brutal to animals. La Fontaine said of the philosophers and logicians of Port-Royal: "They administered beatings to dogs with perfect indifference, and made fun of those who pitied the creatures, as if they had felt pain. They said that the animals

Presidential Address delivered before the Sixty-ninth Annual Eastern Meeting of the American Philosophical Association in Boston, December 28, 1972.
1. Zeno Vendler, *Res Cogitans* (Ithaca, N.Y., 1972), p. 152.
2. *Descartes: Philosophical Letters*, ed. and trans. Anthony Kenny (Oxford, 1970) [hereafter *DL*], p. 53; *Oeuvres de Descartes*, ed. C. Adam and P. Tannery [hereafter AT], II 39. See also *DL*, 243; AT V, 276.

were clocks, that the cries they emitted when struck, were only the noise of a little spring that had been touched, but that the whole body was without feeling." [3] Descartes himself remarks on this point that "my opinion is not so much cruel to animals as indulgent to men . . . since it absolves them from the suspicion of crime when they eat or kill animals." [4]

It is worth noting that in a letter to Henry More, Descartes says that it cannot be *proved* that there is no "thought in animals," because "the human mind does not reach into their hearts." [5] This is a surprising remark, considering his view that thoughts are noncorporeal and nonspatial. Why does he speak as if the issue were one of what is *inside* the animals? Was it a metaphor? The reference to "hearts" (*corda*) is certainly metaphorical. But the idea that our minds cannot look into the animals to determine whether or not any thoughts are there does not seem to be *just* metaphor, since it is offered as an *explanation* (*quia:* because) of why we cannot *prove* that animals do not think. In this same letter Descartes sets forth his "main reason" for holding that animals are without thought— namely, that they do not use "real speech." "Such speech," he says, "is the only certain sign of thought hidden in a body." [6] In another letter to More he expresses himself in the same way, saying that only speech shows thought hidden in a body (*in corpore latentem*).[7] Previously I quoted a passage in which he spoke of the soul as being an "interior" principle. My impression is that, although Descartes' formal position is that soul (or mind) and thought are completely nonspatial and so could not be inside or outside of anything, nevertheless he was actually much influenced by the common metaphysical picture of thought as occurring *inside* a person— of thought as being something *inner*.

In maintaining that animals do not think, Descartes certainly

3. L. C. Rosenfield, *From Beast-Machine to Man-Machine* (New York, 1941), p. 54.

4. *DL* 245; AT V, 278.

5. *DL* 244; AT V, 276–277 (*quia mens humana illorum corda non pervadit*).

6. *DL* 245: AT V, 278 (*Haec enim loquela unicum est cogitationis in corpore latentis signum certum*).

7. *DL* 251; AT V, 345.

meant that they do not reflect or meditate; but did he also mean that they do not have feelings, sensations, or any kind of consciousness? We know from *Meditation II* that to feel (*sentire*) is to think (*cogitare*).[8] Thus if animals don't think they don't feel. In his *Passions of the Soul* Descartes states that nothing ought to be attributed to the soul except thoughts, and that these are of two kinds, actions and passions.[9] Since passions are thoughts, and animals don't have thoughts, therefore they don't have passions, such as fear or anger.

On the other hand, in one of the letters to More, Descartes says that he does *not* deny "sensation" to animals, "in so far as it depends on a bodily organ."[10] In a letter to the Marquess of Newcastle he says that dogs, horses, and monkeys sometimes "express passions" such as fear, hope and joy.[11] Yet, in still another letter, he says that animals do not have "real feeling" or "real passion" (*vray sentiment, vray passion*).[12]

In order to see how these apparent contradictions are to be removed, we need a clear understanding of what Descartes means by a "thought." In an important and difficult passage in *Meditation III* he says:

> Some of my thoughts are, as it were, images of things; the name of "idea" belongs properly to those alone: as when I think of a man, or a chimaera, or heaven, or an angel, or God. But other thoughts have other forms besides: as when I will, when I fear, and when I affirm, when I deny, I do indeed always apprehend something as the object of my thought, yet in the thought I add something else to the idea of that thing; and some of these thoughts are called volitions or affections, and others judgments.[13]

Descartes is saying, I believe, that in every instance of thinking there is, first and foremost, an *idea*. By an "idea" he means a *representation:* this is why he calls it an "image." It is the first form of "thought." As he is using the term "idea" in this passage, an idea

8. *Philosophical Works of Descartes*, ed. and trans. E. Haldane and G. Ross [hereafter HR], I, 153: AT VII, 28.

9. *Passions* I, 17 (HR I, 340; AT XI, 342).   10. *DL* 245; AT V, 278.
11. *DL* 206–207; AT IV, 574–575.   12. *DL* 54; AT II, 41.
13. HR I, 159; AT VII, 37.

would appear to be what is usually meant by a "proposition" or a "propositional content," since ideas, he says, can be affirmed or denied. The idea of God, for example, might be expressed by the sentence "There is a Supremely Perfect Being" or by the nominalized phrase "the existence of a Supremely Perfect Being." In either case, what was expressed could be affirmed or denied.

The second form of "thought" of which Descartes speaks in this passage is not propositional content, but is some "attitude" taken toward propositional content—for example, an attitude of affirming, or denying, or wanting, or fearing, or hoping. One could affirm or deny that a Supremely Perfect Being exists, or want this to be so, or hope or fear that it is so. The kernel of every mental operation is a proposition, i.e., an idea, i.e., a thought in the *first* sense. A thought in the second sense is what nowadays is variously called a "propositional attitude," or a "mental frame." [14]

This conception of what is involved in all "mental operations" has been popular with philosophers. Bertrand Russell subscribed to it in *The Analysis of Mind*. According to him a propositional content could be expressed by the phrase "an egg for breakfast." A person might take different attitudes toward this content: expect it, remember it, merely "entertain" it, desire it, or feel aversion to it. [15] C. I. Lewis had the same conception. The propositional content expressed by the phrase "Mary making pies now" can be the object of different "moods of entertainment": it can be asserted, denied, questioned, postulated, approved, and so on. [16]

The passage from *Meditation III*, previously cited, reveals how Descartes conceived of what might be called "the mental side" of an emotion such as fear. "When I fear," he says, I apprehend something (that is, I "take in" some particular propositional content—for example, that there is a danger confronting me). Then I apply to this propositional content the mental frame or attitude of fearing. If

14. "Mental frame" is Vendler's phrase: *Res Cogitans*, p. 167.
15. Russell, *The Analysis of Mind* (New York, 1921), p. 243.
16. C. I. Lewis, *An Analysis of Knowledge and Valuation* (La Salle, In., 1946), pp. 48–55.

I met a lion in the jungle I would have, according to Descartes, two forms of thought. The first would be a representation, i.e., a propositional content, such as might be expressed by the sentence "The lion may attack me." The second form of thought might be the mental frame of fear. The union of these two forms of thought might be expressed by the sentence "I fear that the lion may attack me."

What else would be involved in my perception and fear of the lion? There would be something purely physical: the physical stimulation of my sensory organs; some physiological changes in heart, brain, nerves, glands; and some avoidance behavior, e.g., running. On Descartes' view the connection between the sensory stimulation and the behavior would be entirely mechanical, unless there was an intervention of the will to prevent the behavior. As Anthony Kenny says, "In its essentials the theory is that the physiological processes involved in the perception of a fearful object, set in motion, by purely mechanical causation, a further physiological process which issues in the behavior characteristic of fear." [17] In one of his letters to More, Descartes says, "Even in us all the motions of the members which accompany our passions are caused not by the soul but simply by the machinery of the body." [18] If a dog met a lion in the jungle his reaction might appear to be like mine. The sensory stimulation, the physiological processes, and the resulting behavior could be quite similar. But for the dog there would be no propositional content and no propositional attitude. There would be no "thought," in either sense of the word, and therefore nothing of the "mental" aspect of fear. When confronted by a fearful object the dog responds purely as a machine. Descartes gives examples of our own human behavior that he regards as machine performances:

If someone quickly thrusts his hand against our eyes as if to strike us, even though we know him to be our friend, that he only does it in fun, and that he will take great care not to hurt us, we have, all the same, trouble in preventing ourselves from closing them, and this shows that it is not by

17. Anthony Kenny, *Action, Emotion and Will* (New York, 1963), p. 8.
18. *DL* 251; AT V, 345.

the intervention of our soul that they close . . . but it is because the machine of our body is so formed that the movement of this hand towards our eyes excites another movement in our brain which conducts the animal spirits into the muscles which cause the eyelids to close.[19]

It becomes clear why Descartes said, on the one hand, that animals have feeling and passion but, on the other hand, that they do not have "real" feeling and passion. The propositional representations and attitudes that are produced in people by sensory stimulations and physiological processes do not occur in the "lower" animals. For the same reason, the animals do not have *sensation* in the full sense. Descartes wrote to More that "thought is included in our mode of sensation." [20] He meant the *human* mode of sensation. If every human sensation includes thought, and if thought is propositional content together with propositional attitude, then at the center of every sensation of ours there is a proposition. Animals do not have propositional thoughts and therefore do not have sensations in the human mode.

In first reading Descartes it surprises one that he should include emotion, feeling, and sensation under "thinking." But this would be a natural employment of the word "thinking," given his conception of the propositional nature of human emotion, feeling, and sensation.

In the *Reply to Objections VI* Descartes distinguishes between three "grades" of sensation:

To the first [grade] belongs the immediate affection of the bodily organ by external objects; and this can be nothing else than the motion of the particles of the sensory organs and the change of figure and position due to that motion. The second [grade] comprises the immediate mental results, due to the mind's union with the corporeal organ affected; such are the perceptions of pain, of pleasurable stimulation, of thirst, of hunger, of colours, of sound, savour, odour, cold, heat, and the like. . . . Finally the third [grade] contains all those judgments which, on the occasion of mo-

19. *Passions*, I, 13 (HR I, 338; AT XI, 338–339). "Animal spirits" are minute bodies that move at high speed.
20. *DL* 244; AT V, 277 (*in nostro sentiendi modo cogitatio includitur*).

tions occurring in the corporeal organ, we have from our earliest years been accustomed to pass about things external to us.[21]

The first grade of sensation is shared by animals and people. It is the only sense in which animals have sensation. The second grade involves perceptions (*perceptiones*) of pain, heat, cold, sound, and so on. On Descartes' view this grade of sensation involves propositional content, and so is *thinking*. Presumably the propositional content of a sensation of heat in the second grade would be expressed by the sentence "It seems to me that I feel heat." In *Meditation II* he presents such an occurrence as its seeming to him that he feels heat as an example of what is properly called sensation or feeling (*sentire*); and he declares that it is "nothing other than thinking" (*cogitare*).[22] I suppose that the propositional content of a sensation of pain would be "I feel pain." In a letter to Mersenne, Descartes actually says that "pain exists only in the understanding" (*la douleur n'est que dans l'entendement*), and that animals don't have pain.[23] It appears that in order to have a pain one must apprehend and affirm a proposition. In the *Principles,* Descartes says that my sensation (*sensu*) of seeing or of walking is "my consciously seeming to see or to walk": this "refers only to my mind, which alone is concerned with my feeling or thinking that I see and I walk." [24] Descartes' third grade of sensation is called "thinking" because it consists of "customary judgments" about the material world—for example, that there is a source of heat nearby; that it is the burn on my arm that is giving me pain; that I am walking.

How does Descartes conceive the relation between thought and consciousness? He says, "By the word 'thought' I understand all those things that are in us consciously, in so far as we are conscious of them." [25] Something is a thought of mine if and only if I am conscious of it, and only to the extent I am conscious of it. Con-

---

21. *HR* II, 251; AT VII, 436–437.   22. *HR* I, 153; AT VII, 29.
23. AT III, 85.   24. *Principles* I, 9 (HR I, 222; AT VIII, 7–8).
25. *Principles* I, 9 (HR I, 222; AT VIII, 7: *Cogitationis nomine, intellego illa omnia, quae nobis consciis in nobis sunt, quatenus eorum in nobis conscientia est*).

sciousness requires thought—that is propositional content. Since animals have no thought they have no consciousness of anything.

Although Zeno Vendler's interpretations of Descartes are admirable, here I want to pick a slight quarrel with him. He seems to think that Descartes' identification of "thoughts" with "all those things that are in us consciously" led him into the mistake of regarding sensations as thoughts, since we are conscious of sensations. According to Vendler our actual concept of thought is restricted to mental acts and states that have propositional content. He believes that Descartes "never succeeded in catching this distinction"—that is, the distinction between mental states that have propositional content and those that do not. Vendler says that "instead of the specific distinction between the propositional and the nonpropositional, all he (Descartes) sees is a difference of degree between the clear and the confused." [26]

According to my understanding, however, Descartes was precisely insisting that when we mean by "sensation" something other than mere physiological processes, then sensation does have propositional content. Indeed, I suggest that for Descartes the distinction between the "mental" and the "physical" is *defined* by the presence or absence of propositional content. In the *Passions* he says that "there is nothing in us that we ought to attribute to our soul excepting our thoughts," and he adds, as we previously noted, that thoughts are of two sorts, actions and passions.[27] Actions are volitions (*volontez*). According to the analysis of *Meditation III*, a volition consists of an *idea*, i.e., a propositional content, together with the attitude or mental frame of willing that content. Similarly, a passion is a propositional content, plus the attitude of fearing, or hoping, and so on. Thus *everything* properly attributed to soul or mind is propositional.

As Vendler notes, bodily sensations are regarded by Descartes as "confused modes of thought." Descartes says, "For all these sensations of hunger, thirst, pain etc., are in truth none other than cer-

26. Vendler, p. 155.   27. *Passions*, I, 17 (HR I, 340; AT XI, 342).

tain confused modes of thought which are produced by the union and apparent intermingling of mind and body." [28] What is the nature of the "confusion" in this mode of thought? According to Descartes it is a *conceptual* confusion. We have a natural inclination to assume that when we feel pain in our foot, there actually is a sensation in our foot—as if a *sensation* could be located *in one's foot!* We can, however, purge ourselves of that confusion. We can arrive at a clear understanding of what a pain is. Descartes says that "we have a clear or distinct knowledge of pain, colour, and other things of the sort when we consider them simply as sensations or thoughts" (*sensus sive cogitationes*). [29] When I succeed in regarding a pain of mine as nothing else than a sensation, that is to say, as *a thought*, I shall be freed of my former conceptual blunder—since I cannot suppose that there is *a thought in my foot!*

Probably I shall regard *in-my-foot* as a quality of the sensation (just as *throbbing* can be a quality of a sensation). Certainly I shall not regard "in-my-foot" as specifying a physical location of my sensation! Regardless, however, of whether or not I attain to that stage of supposed conceptual clarity the fact is, according to Descartes, that the pain-in-my-foot is a thought! It consists of a propositional content (which might be expressed by the phrase "My having an in-my-foot pain"), plus the mental frame of affirming, joined (no doubt) by the mental frame of dislike. If I wince, cry out, or limp, this has nothing to do with the sensation as such, but is solely a performance of my bodily machine.

According to my understanding of Descartes, he explicitly and consciously adopted the position that there is a propositional kernel in every feeling, desire, voluntary act, emotion, and sensation. this is why he could hold that his essential nature consists solely in being a thinking thing. [30] It was *not* because he employed *cogitare* and *penser* in an eccentrically broad way that he listed imagining, sensation, and emotion under "thinking." It was because he be-

28. *Meditation VI* (HR I, 192; AT VII, 81).
29. *Principles* I, 68 (HR I, 248; AT VIII, 33). See also *Principles* I, 67.
30. *Meditation VI* (HR I, 190; AT VII, 78).

lieved that every "mental operation" consists in taking an attitude towards a proposition.

In my opinion this is an absurdly overintellectualized view of the life of man. It helps us to understand, however, why Descartes thought that animals are automatons. They are devoid of mind, of all consciousness and awareness, of real feeling and sensation, because they do not "apprehend," "entertain," "contemplate," or, in plain language, think of *propositions*.

II

In real life we commonly employ the verb "think" in respect to animals. We say, "Towser thinks he is going to be fed," just as naturally as we say, "Towser wants to be fed." Suppose our dog is chasing the neighbor's cat. The latter runs full tilt toward an oak tree, but suddenly swerves at the last moment and disappears up a nearby maple. The dog doesn't see this maneuver, and on arriving at the oak tree he rears up on his hind legs, paws the trunk as if trying to scale it, and barks excitedly into the branches above. We who observe the whole episode from a window say, "He thinks that the cat went up that oak tree." We say, "thinks" because he is barking up the wrong tree. If the cat *had* gone up the oak tree and if the dog's performance had been the same, we could have said, "He knows that the cat went up the oak." But let us stay with "thinks." A million examples could be produced in which it would be a correct way of speaking to say, of an animal, something of the form "He thinks that *p*." Clearly there is an error in Descartes' contention that animals do not think.

Let us, however, take note of a distinction. In commenting later on the incident of the dog and the cat we could, without any qualms, say of our dog, "He thought that the cat went up the oak tree." We should, in contrast, feel reluctant and embarrassed to say "He had the thought that the cat went up the oak tree." In referring to an animal it is natural enough to say "He thought that *p*," but not "He had the thought that *p*." It would sound funny to say of a dog, monkey, or dolphin, that the thought that *p* occurred to

him, or struck him, or went through his mind. All of us are familiar with the sort of evidence on the basis of which we predicate of
animals (or rather, of *some* animals) that they think that so-and-so;
but we are not familiar with any basis for attributing *thoughts* to
them.

Apparently Descartes did not catch this distinction between "to
think" and "to have thoughts." In his first letter to Henry More, he
says it is a prejudice to suppose that "dumb animals think" (*bruta
animantia cogitare*); and then he goes on to give his reasons for holding that "beasts lack thought" (*bestias cogitatione destitutas esse*).[31] He
is treating "to think" and "to have thoughts" as if they are equivalent: but we have seen that they are not.[32]

One way of stating the significance of this distinction is to say
that although we apply the word "think" to animals, using it as a
transitive verb taking a propositional phrase as its object, we do not
thereby imply that the animal *formulated* or *thought of* a proposition,
or had a proposition "before its mind." In saying something about
the animal, we employ a verb that, grammatically, takes a propositional expression as object, without meaning that as a matter of
psychological fact the animal thought of a proposition or thought
via a proposition.

The next point to see is that we employ the verb "think" in the
same way in regard to *people*. On the basis of circumstances and behavior we say that a man "thought that *p*," without implying that
he thought *of p* or formulated *p*, or that *p* occurred to him or was in
his thoughts. For example, suppose a friend of mine and I are
engrossed in an exciting conversation. We are about to drive off in
his car. While holding up his end of the conversation he fumbles in
his pocket for the car keys. I, knowing that they are in the glove
compartment, say to myself, "He thinks the keys are in his

31. *DL* 243, 244; AT V, 276, 278.

32. Vendler points out (*Res Cogitans*, pp. 198–199) that Descartes sometimes uses
cogitare as a transitive, propositional verb—that is, as meaning "to think that *p*." One
of several examples Vendler cites is *cogitem me videre*, which can be translated as "I
think I see" or "I think that I see" (HR I, 156; AT VII, 33).

pocket." I do not imply that he said to himself, or thought to himself, "The keys are in my pocket." Grammatical form is no index of psychological reality.

I am aware that the example of my friend fumbling in his pocket and, even more so, the example of the dog clawing the tree, produce philosophical discomfort. How can it be correct to say that my friend "thinks" the keys are in his pocket, when he isn't having any thoughts about the keys? How can it be correct to say that the dog "thinks" the cat went up the oak tree, in face of the fact that a dog cannot rightly be said to have thoughts about anything? There is a halfhearted inclination to *deny* that it is really correct to say those things. Here I simply appeal to ordinary language. It is clearly right to use "thinks" in both cases.[33]

The next move to relieve the discomfort is more interesting. There is an inclination to suppose that what we *mean* when we say, as in my example, "He thinks the keys are in his pocket" is "He *acts as if* he had the thought 'The keys are in my pocket'." Likewise, the dog *acts as if* he had the thought "That confounded cat went up this tree."

33. In a recent essay Donald Davidson overlooks the distinction between *thinking that p* and *having the thought that p*. He says: "We attribute a thought to a creature whenever we assertively employ a positive sentence the main verb of which is psychological—in English, 'believes', 'knows', 'hopes', 'desires', 'thinks', 'fears', 'is interested' are examples—followed by a sentence and preceded by the name or description of the creature" (Donald Davidson, "Thought and Talk," *Mind and Language*, ed. S. Guttenplan [Oxford, 1975], p. 8). The case of the dog of whom we do say, "He thought that the cat went up the oak tree," but of whom we are unwilling to say, "He had the thought that the cat went up the oak tree," is a plain counterexample. And when I say (to myself) of my human friend who is groping for his keys, "He thinks the keys are in his pocket," I do not *thereby* attribute to him *the thought* that the keys are in his pocket. Davidson also expresses the opinion that a creature cannot "have a belief if it does not have the *concept* of belief" (ibid., p. 22; emphasis added). Now it is true that I would hesitate to say of the dog that it "has the belief" that the cat went up the oak tree; but I would say, without any hesitation, that it "believes" that the cat went up the oak tree; and it would be absurd to suppose that the dog has the concept of belief, for the reason given by Davidson, namely, that "a creature must be a member of a speech community if it is to have the concept of belief" (ibid.). Evidently, a creature can believe that *p*, or think that *p*, without being a member of a speech community.

This is an interesting move because it reveals a tendency to regard *having thoughts* as the prototype or the paradigm of *thinking*. Other uses of "thinks" are felt to be derivative from, or parasitic on, this prototype. If those uses somehow refer to, or converge on, the prototype, they are intelligible; otherwise not.

I believe this idea is mistaken. There is *nothing* that deserves to be regarded as *the* paradigm or prototype of thinking. There are many paradigms of thinking, no one of which holds a central place in the application of the word. Just as there is nothing that is *the* prototype of *furniture*. There are different kinds of furniture, and different forms of thinking, none being furniture or thinking *par excellence*. There are connections between the different forms of thinking; but this does not mean that there is an essential nature of thinking, or that the forms of thinking converge towards a center. There is no reason to believe that the concept of thinking has that kind of unity.

Just why there is an especially strong urge to select the phenomenon of having thoughts as being that which lies at the center is a fascinating problem into which I will not venture. I limit myself to remarking that there is no warrant for believing that there is *a center*, occupied by anything.

Let us return to the observation that the formula "He thought that *p*" does not entail the formula "The thought that *p* occurred to him." The same holds for a host of propositional verbs. You and I notice, for example, that Robinson is walking in a gingerly way, and you ask why. I reply, "Because he realizes that the path is slippery." I do not imply that the proposition "This path is slippery" crossed his mind. Another example: I wave at a man across the quad. Later on I may say to someone, "I saw Kaspar today." It may be true that I recognized Kaspar, or recognized that the man across the quad was Kaspar, but not true that I thought to myself, "That is Kaspar." Turning from propositional verbs to emotions and sensations, it is plainly false that whenever a man is angry he thinks of the proposition "I am angry," or that whenever he feels a pain in his leg the thought "I have a pain in my leg" occurs to him. Descartes was wrong in holding that "our mode of sensation includes thought." Human sensation does not always, or even characteristically, include thought.

Noting these facts should help us to see that the gap between ourselves and at least the higher of the lower animals is not as great as Descartes supposed. His distorted view of the matter was in part the result of his doctrine that human mental phenomena are always propositional. His claim that his essential nature is thinking is actually the claim that his essential nature consists in *thinking of propositions*. When we see the enormity of this exaggeration of the propositional in human life, our unwillingness to ascribe propositional thinking to animals ought no longer to make us refuse to attribute to them a panoply of forms of feeling, of perception, of realization, of recognition, that are, more often than not, nonpropositional in the human case. Their nonpropositional character does *not* mark them as something less than real forms of consciousness.

III

Still, there is a gap between animals and humans, as is revealed by our reluctance to attribute thoughts to animals. Once I owned an Airedale dog who hated a bath, and it came about in the course of time that whenever he saw preparations for a bath underway he would go into hiding. I have no hesitation in saying that he "realized" he was going to be given a bath, or in saying that he had "learned from experience" that certain preparations were followed by a bath. (Whether or not this adds up to his being "rational" I won't try to say.) But certainly I would not attribute to him the thought "Here we go again! Another of those horrible baths."

In this regard I would take a stronger position than Descartes did. He said it could not be *proved* either that animals do or that they do not have thoughts "hidden in their bodies," thus conceding it to be *possible* that they do have thoughts after all. But the idea that we cannot determine whether dogs have thoughts *in* them is a dreadful confusion. Suppose we did know everything that is hidden in their bodies: how could we tell which of these things were thoughts?

The notion that dogs may have hidden thoughts is a red herring. The relevant question is whether they *express* thoughts. I think the answer is clearly in the negative. Let us go back to Robinson who is walking on a slippery path. Just from his gingerly movements we know he is aware that the footing is slippery; but we cannot determine from this character of his movements whether the thought "This path is slippery" has occurred to him. In the case of a person we can often find out whether the thought that p crossed his mind, either by overhearing him *say* that p, or by his subsequently *testifying* that the thought that p occurred to him. With animals we don't have either recourse. The possession of language makes the whole difference. If a dog on that slippery path moved in an equally gingerly way, we could say with propriety that the dog is aware that the path is slippery. What further thing could we do to find out whether the thought "This path is slippery" occurred to it, or crossed its mind? An undertaking of trying to find out whether the dog did or didn't have that thought is not anything we understand.

Descartes' notion was that speech is the only "sign" of the presence of thought. This suggests, as I have said, that just conceivably animals may have thoughts of which they give no sign. This implies a looseness of connection between thought and the linguistic expression of thought that is deeply disturbing. It conveys the picture of two kinds of processes, sometimes running more or less parallel, one consisting of the linguistic expression of thoughts, the other consisting of the thoughts themselves. This picture, if taken seriously, ought to create an uncertainty as to whether *people* have thoughts. If thoughts are states or processes that linguistic utterances are supposed to match, then how can one be sure that the right matchings are made, or any matchings at all, not only in the case of other people, but in one's own case too? The relationship between language and thought must be closer than that: so close that it is really senseless to conjecture that people may *not* have thoughts, and also really senseless to conjecture that animals *may* have thoughts.

Thoughts cannot, of course, be identified with sentences: they are not linguistic entities. Nor can thoughts be identified with the uttering of sentences. Nor can they be identified with behavioral propensities. Nor with physiological events. Nor can they be identified with a flow of bodily sensations and images. What are they then?

This is a strange question. Why should we even be moved to ask what thoughts are, in general? Given a certain context we often know what particular thought a particular man had. For example, McCarthy always takes the 7:30 bus to work, but this morning he was late and missed it. On returning to the house he says to his wife, "This may cause me to lose my job." We know what his thought was. What can be said, other than that his thought was that he might lose his job? What makes us suppose there might be some other kind of answer? It is only from the vantage, or disadvantage, of a philosophical theory, such as a monolithic behaviorism, or a monolithic materialism, that it can seem to us that another sort of answer is in the offing.

We need to avoid identifying thoughts with their linguistic expression. At the same time we should reject the suggestion that it is *possible* that language-less creatures should have thoughts. The case is somewhat analogous to the fact that mirror images are not identical with mirrors, yet it is impossible that there should be mirror images without mirrors. The analogy fails in the following respect: it is possible that a person should have had a certain thought at time *t*, even though no linguistic expression of that thought occurred at *t*. Whereas it is impossible that a mirror image should exist at *t* unless a mirroring surface existed at *t*. But this disanalogy does not argue an independence of thought from language: for it is meaningful to suppose that a person might have had a thought to which he gave no expression, only because this person speaks or spoke a language in which there is an institution of testifying to previously unexpressed thoughts.

I agree, therefore, with the Cartesians that thoughts cannot be attributed to animals that are without language. But I come here not to praise men for their thoughts, but to defend animals from their Cartesian and Neo-Cartesian detractors. These philosophers say that animals do not have "minds." People quarrel profoundly over the question of whether cats are more or less intelligent than dogs. Could cats be more intelligent than dogs but still not have minds? Of some animals we can say that they are frightened, joyous, affectionate; that they want, seek, pursue, hide, lie in wait, play, tease, defend; that they see, hear, smell, like, dislike, avoid; that they remember, recognize, realize, and think. Despite all this and more, don't they have minds? It is hard to get a grip on the question.

Descartes says that a mind is something that thinks: in this case both I and my dog *are* minds, for both of us may think that the cat went up the oak tree. I have tried to show, however, that Descartes mistakenly equates thinking with having thoughts.[34] His view is that a "mind" is something that has thoughts. Now, *I* have thoughts, but my poor doggy has none. So *I* am a mind but he is not. The latter-day Cartesian, Zeno Vendler, says that "To have a mind is to have thoughts." [35] If this is true, then my dog neither is nor has a mind. But we should understand what this comes to— just that he doesn't have thoughts: which in turn comes to just this, that he doesn't have a language. We can appreciate, however, that despite this the dog isn't so badly off, since a great range of feelings, sensations, wants, perceptions, and realizings can be accurately attributed to him.

34. This Cartesian view is so commonly held that some philosophers regard it as a truism. For example, in a recent number of *Mind*, Justus Hartnack says: "It may be maintained, *although a bit trivially*, that thinking consists of thoughts. Thinking is the stream of thoughts" ("On Thinking," *Mind*, 81 [1972], 550: my italics). Hartnack also takes a Cartesian position in declaring that "there can be no thoughts and no thinking if there is no language" (ibid., p. 551). I am urging that once we acknowledge the distinction between thinking and having thoughts, then we can see that if there were no language thinking could occur, but no one could have thoughts.
35. Vendler, p. 187.

What about consciousness? A dog, like a man, can be knocked unconscious. But if a dog runs around, barks, and picks a fight with another dog, isn't he conscious? We saw that Descartes ties consciousness exclusively to thoughts. Although Vendler believes Descartes was mistaken in regarding animals as automatons, he inclines to interpret consciousness in the same narrow way that Descartes did, namely, as consisting solely in having thoughts. Vendler says: "If . . . consciousness be defined as the totality of one's thoughts (at a given moment), then sensations and feelings do not enter consciousness until by noticing or being aware of them one forms or entertains a perceptual judgment. If this is true, then we must agree with Descartes that animals, strictly speaking, cannot be conscious of their sensations and other experiences." [36] But isn't there a great deal of human consciousness that doesn't involve thoughts or propositional content? I stop my car at an intersection because the light is red. I was aware of the red light and was also aware that the light was red. Did I think to myself, "That light is red"? Probably not. Or suppose that as you pass an acquaintance he says "Hello" to you, and you respond in kind. Did you think to yourself, "He said, 'Hello' "? Suppose you did not. Would it be true, therefore, that you were not conscious of his greeting? Of course not.

There are many forms of human response that manifest consciousness of objects, situations and events; and animals share in some of these forms of consciousness. Descartes says that this belief is due to a pervasive prejudice. I think the shoe is on the other foot. It is the prejudice of philosophers that only propositional thoughts belong to consciousness which stands in the way of our perceiving the continuity of consciousness between human and animal life.

36. Ibid., p. 162.

3 | *Descartes' Proof that He Is Essentially a Non-Material Thing*

1. Having thought to have proved his own existence by the *cogito* argument, Descartes goes on to claim that his nature consists solely in being a thinking thing, and also that he is essentially a non-material thing. These claims have puzzled students of Descartes. First, by what reasoning did he think he had established that his nature consisted solely in being a thinking thing? Second, how did he think he had established that he was essentially a non-material thing? Many philosophers would regard these two conclusions as incompatible. Gassendi or Hobbes would hold that a thinking thing necessarily is a material thing.

I will leave aside the first problem.[1] I will limit myself here to considering whether Descartes has a sound proof, or what might plausibly appear to be a sound proof, that he is essentially a non-material thing.

The most famous of Descartes' arguments to prove this conclusion is his so-called argument from doubt. It employs the following premises:[2]

> I cannot doubt that I exist.
> I can doubt that I have a body.

1. I speculate about this problem in my essay, "Descartes' Proof that His Essence Is Thinking," *Philosophical Review*, 74 (1965), republished as the first essay in the present volume.

2. For a review of the Cartesian texts in which the argument from doubt occurs, and also for criticisms of the argument, see Sections 11 and 12 of the above essay.

Descartes expresses in different ways the conclusion he draws from these premises. In *The Search After Truth* the conclusion is "I am not a body." [3] He uses basically the same argument twice in the *Principles*. [4] In the first of these two occurrences his conclusion is "Body does not pertain to my nature"; in the second it is "I am distinct from material substance." In the *Notae in Programma* the conclusion is expressed like this: "The concept of mind does not involve any concept of body." [5]

What Descartes holds is that from the fact that he cannot doubt that he exists but can doubt that he has a body, and can even doubt that any material thing at all exists, it follows that there is no logically necessary or essential connection between his existence and the existence of any material thing. The reasoning, however, is fallacious. It is easy to construct an argument of substantially the same form that is obviously invalid. (See note 2.)

2. I had supposed for some years that Descartes had no valid reasoning on this matter. Fairly recently I discovered this not to be so. In a preliminary draft of a paper he kindly sent to me, Robert Jaeger conjectured that Descartes might have employed the valid argument that I am about to formulate. An examination of some Cartesian texts confirmed Jaeger's conjecture. It is worthwhile to focus attention on the argument, both for its intrinsic philosophical interest and also because it has, to the best of my knowledge, escaped the notice of the learned commentators.

Consider the following form of deductive reasoning:

p entails q
p does not entail r
Therefore, q does not entail r

3. *Philosophical Works of Descartes*, ed. and trans. E. Haldane and G. Ross, I, 319; *Oeuvres de Descartes*, ed. C. Adam and P. Tannery, X, 518.
4. *Principles of Philosophy*, Pt. I; Principles 7, 8; Principle 60 (HR I, 221, 244; AT VIII, 6–7, 29).
5. HR I, 440; AT VIII, 354.

This is a valid form. Now substitute for *p* the proposition *I think I am breathing;* for *q* the proposition *I exist;* for *r* the proposition *I have a body.* This yields the following instantiation:

> *I think I am breathing* entails *I exist.*
> *I think I am breathing* does not entail *I have a body.*
> Therefore, *I exist* does not entail *I have a body.*

In a letter that Descartes wrote to Reneri in 1638 there is the following passage:

> When someone says 'I am breathing, therefore I am' if he wants to prove he exists from the fact that there cannot be breathing without existence, he proves nothing, because he would have to prove first that it is true that he is breathing, which is impossible unless he has also proved that he exists. But if he wants to prove his existence from the feeling or opinion that he has that he is breathing, so that he judges that even if the opinion was untrue he could not have it if he did not exist, then his proof is sound. For in such a case the thought of breathing is present to our mind before the thought of our existing, and we cannot doubt that we have it while we have it. To say 'I am breathing, therefore I am', in this sense, is simply to say 'I am thinking, therefore I am'. You will find on examination that all other propositions from which we can thus prove our existence reduce to the same one; so that one cannot prove from them the existence of the body, i.e., of a nature which occupies space, etc., but only that of the soul, i.e., of a nature which thinks. [6]

In this passage the argument I formulated is implicit, even though the focus of Descartes' attention is elsewhere.

In his *Reply to Objections V*, Descartes, responding to the charge that he did not need the "elaborate machinery" of the *cogito* to prove his own existence, makes the foregoing argument quite explicit:

> When you say that I could have inferred the same conclusion from any of my other actions, you wander far from the truth, because there is none of my activities of which I am wholly certain (in the sense of having metaphysical certitude, which alone is here involved), save thinking alone. For

---

6. *Descartes: Philosophical Letters*, ed. and trans. Anthony Kenny, p. 52; AT II, 37–38.

example you have no right to make the inference: *I walk, hence I exist*, except in so far as our awareness of walking is a thought; it is of this alone that the inference holds good, not of the motion of the body, which sometimes does not exist, as in dreams, when nevertheless I appear to walk. Hence from the fact that I think that I walk I can very well infer the existence of the mind which so thinks, but not that of the body which walks. So it is also in all other cases.[7]

In this passage the following propositions are set out plainly enough:

> *I think I am walking* entails *I exist*.
> *I think I am walking* does not entail *I have a body*.

From the conjunction of these two propositions it follows that

> *I exist* does not entail *I have a body*.

Descartes does not state, in so many words, that this conclusion is a valid inference from those two premises; but it would be safe to assume that he was aware of it.

3. I am using the words "entails" in a sense in which it has been widely employed in philosophy and logic. Considering it solely in its application to contingent propositions, to say that *p* "entails" *q* is equivalent to saying that the conjunction, *p and not-q*, is self-contradictory. This is commonly regarded as equivalent to the following formulation: It is "logically *im*possible" that *p* should be true when *q* is false. Accordingly, to say that *p* does *not* entail *q* is equivalent to saying that it is "logically *possible*" that *p* should be true when *q* is false.

What Descartes' valid reasoning purports to prove is that it is logically possible that he, or I, or anyone who states the argument, should exist without a body: in other words, that it it logically possible that the conjunction, *I exist and I do not have a body*, should be true. One can also say that the conclusion is *I am not a material thing;* but this could be misleading. Descartes did not, of course,

---

7. HR II, 207; AT VII, 352.

aim to prove that he was not a material thing in the sense of not *in fact* having a body. He did intend to prove that he was not *necessarily* a material thing—that it was not logically (or "metaphysically") necessary for his existence that he should have a material body. Sometimes I express the conclusion of Descartes' argument in the words "I am not a material thing," sometimes in the words "I am essentially a non-material thing." In either case what I mean is that Descartes aimed to prove by this argument the following proposition: *It is logically possible that I should exist without a body.*

4.   Descartes often represented himself as having established that *mind* or *soul* is not corporeal. The argument we are considering has as its conclusion that *I* am not a material thing, not that *my mind* is not a material thing. Hobbes, Gassendi, and some present-day materialists hold that my mind *is* a material thing. ("The mind is the brain.") How does Descartes arrive at the conclusion that *my mind* is not a material thing? Two points should be mentioned here. First, Descartes regards it as a matter of definition that "mind" is "that which thinks." A thinking thing is a "mind, " by definition. Secondly, by reasoning that is hard to unravel, Descartes thought he had proved that his essential nature consisted solely in being a thinking thing. For him, that is equivalent to proving that he is essentially a mind and nothing more. This is why he *identifies I* or *me* with *my mind* or *my soul*, in both *Discourse* and *Meditations:* "this I or me, that is to say, the soul by which I am what I am." [8] We are now ready for the proof that *my mind* is not a material thing:

> I am identical with my mind.
> I am not a material thing.
> Therefore, my mind is not a material thing.

A further point can be mentioned here. Descartes is convinced that he is a thing that has properties—that is, a substance. "I am a substance," he says in the *Meditations*. [9] Now Descartes holds that there

---

8. HR I, 101, 190; AT VII, 33, 78.   9. HR I, 165; AT VII, 44.

are only two kinds of substances, mental and material. If this were accepted, and if one were also to accept the argument (of Section 2) which purports to prove that he is not a material substance, then it has to be accepted that he is a mental substance, i.e., a mind. With these additions, the argument ending in the conclusion that *I exist* does not entail *I have a body* appears to provide the foundation for proving both that *I* am not a material thing and also that *my mind* is not a material thing.

5.   Since the argument referred to in Section 2 is formally valid, any reluctance to accept these conclusions makes it incumbent on one to disagree with one or both of the premises of that argument. Consider first the premise: *I think I am breathing* entails *I exist*. One might object here that "I exist," as employed by Descartes in his soliloquy, is not a meaningful thing to say or think, and therefore that the consequent of the alleged entailment is a non-proposition. I am sympathetic to this criticism. Although one can conceive of circumstances in which "I exist" would be a significant utterance, it is hard to see how it could be when one was merely talking or thinking to oneself in philosophical soliloquy, which is Descartes' supposed situation in the *Meditations*. But the point is a difficult one to argue and I will not pursue it here.

Let us turn to the second premise: *I think I am breathing* does not entail *I have a body*. This is equivalent to: It is logically possible that (at one and the same time) I should think I am breathing and also should not have a body. In other words, the conjunction, "I think I am breathing *and* I do not have a body," is being put forward as a sentence expressing a logical possiblity.

I have a difficulty with the claim that it expresses "a logical possiblity." To make clear my difficulty I will shift my attention from this first-person sentence to its third person counterpart, namely, "He thinks he is breathing *and* he does not have a body." What I am going to do is to question the intelligibility, in a sense, of this latter sentence, and then go back to question the intelligibility of its first-person mate.

One could object that this maneuver of switching to the third person is contrary to the practice and spirit of Descartes' philosophical method in the *Meditations*. I agree. I will discuss this matter more fully later. But for now I want to issue the reminder that in actual language, first-person, third-person pairs are connected in the following way: a first-person statement is true only if its third-person counterpart is true. For example, if right now I were to make the statement "I am six feet tall," my statement would be true *only* if it is the case that were another person to say about me "He is six feet tall," his statement would be true. If his statement were false, my own statement would be false too.

The same thing also holds for all first-person statements or utterances, including those that are commonly called "psychological" by philosophers, such as "I have a headache" or "I am angry at Robinson." If I were to announce now that I am angry at Robinson, my statement would be true *only* if the statement "He is angry at Robinson" that someone other than myself might make about me were true. If that third-person statement was false, my own statement about myself would be false. I am assuming, of course, that the other speaker and myself would be meaning the same thing by "angry," would be using the name "Robinson" to designate the same person, would be referring to the same period of time, and so on.

The general truth-value connection between first-person and third-person pairs can, I believe, be stated as follows: if a first-person statement has a certain truth-value (i.e., is true, or is false) then necessarily its third-person counterpart has the same truth-value. If I say, "I have a headache," and you say of me, "He has a headache," it cannot be that my statement is true and yours is false, nor that yours is true and mine is false.[10]

---

10. I am indebted to Alvin Plantinga for an objection to the universality of my claim that every true first-person statement has a true third-person counterpart. In a discussion at the Oxford Philosophical Society of an earlier version of the present essay, Plantinga produced the following example: There is a nuclear explosion of which I am the sole survivor. I make the true assertion "I am the only person alive."

A cautionary remark should be registerd: some third-person psychological statements do not have legitimate first-person counterparts. If I were knocked unconscious, someone could point at me and make the true statement "He is unconscious." But it does not follow that *I* could appropriately declare or think, "I am unconscious." The sentence "I am unconscious" is a degenerate sentence in the sense that it has no statement-making use in the language.[11] I do not wish to hold that whenever there is a true third-person statement, there is a counterpart first-person statement that is true.

What I do believe to be certainly the case is that whenever anyone makes a meaningful statement about himself in the first person, there is a corresponding third-person statement which could be made by someone else, and which would be true if the first-person statement is true and false if it is false. This is a necessary condition (although, as said above, not a sufficient condition) for a first-person statement or utterance to have a truth-value. This necessary

---

Since there is no other living person then a fortiori, no person other than myself could make about me the true assertion "He is the only person alive."

I am inclined to respond to Plantinga's criticism by holding on to the universality of my claim, but allowing that in the exceptional circumstances imagined, the proper third-person counterpart of my true first-person statement would be a statement in the *past* tense, namely, "He was the only person alive." It is possible, logically speaking, that at a time *subsequent* to the time when I was the only person alive, there should be a living person other than myself, who made this statement, referring to me and to that time when I was the only person alive. Thus, there can be peculiar cases in which first- and third-person counterparts would differ in *tense* although referring to the same time.

My motive for insisting on third-person counterparts for first-person statements is to deny to Descartes, and to like-minded philosophers, the right to assume that the medium in which all one's thinking took place could be a language that was an exclusively first-person language. Descartes' procedure in the *Meditations* requires this assumption. I comment on this matter in Sections 9 and 10.

11. Other examples of sentences that are degenerate in the same way are "I do not exist" and "I am asleep." Taking a suggestion from Jaakko Hintikka, we can say that what is degenerate about such sentences is that they are "self-defeating." Whoever tried to make anyone believe that he is nonexistent, unconscious, or asleep by saying so, in a first-person sentence, would necessarily defeat his own purpose. See Hintikka's paper, *"Cogito, Ergo Sum:* Inference or Performance?", *Philosophical Review*, 71 (1962), especially section 7 and footnote 23.

condition is that its third-person counterpart must have the *same* truth-value. This requirement has the following important corollary: if a particular third-person statement cannot be true, then necessarily its first-person counterpart cannot be true. I will make use of this corollary in my discussion of Descartes' argument.

6.   Let us return to the second premise of his argument. It is:

I think I am breathing does *not* entail *I have a body.*

As previously noted, this premise is equivalent to the statement that it is a logical possibility that the two propositions, *I think I am breathing* and *I have no body*, should be true at the same time. It would follow that it is a logical possibility that the third-person counterparts, *He thinks he is breathing*, and *He has no body*, should be true at the same time.

Let us turn our attention to the conjunction of the two sentences "He thinks he is breathing" and "He has no body." To avoid possible confusion about the scope of "thinks," I will reverse the order of the conjuncts. Thus, we are considering the conjunction: "He has no body and he thinks he is breathing."

This conjunction has a logical peculiarity that makes it doubtful, to my mind, whether it can rightly be said that the conjunction expresses a logical possibility. There is a respect in which the two conjuncts are at odds with one another. The whole conjunction has a queer sort of inconsistency.

To bring out what I mean, let us reflect on the criteria that each of us employs for saying that some other person thinks or believes so and so, or has such and such a thought. We rely heavily on the movements, actions, utterances of that person. If a friend of yours was lying in bed, dangerously ill, you might get him to give signals indicating the condition of his breathing: the rapid blinking of his eyes might mean that he thinks he is no longer breathing; the motion of an index finger might mean that he thinks he is breathing. On observing the later signal you could report, "He thinks he is breathing."

Each of us ascribes various thoughts, beliefs, feelings, emotions, to other people on the basis of their behavior and facial expressions; their nods, grimaces, smiles; their exclamations, outbursts, silences; their approaching, withdrawing, gesturing. Of course the *meaning* of such items of behavior is dependent on the situations in which they occur. But the point is that our ascriptions of thoughts, feelings, beliefs, desires, to other human persons rely on criteria which presuppose that we are ascribing those phenomena to corporeal creatures in a corporeal world. Wittgenstein puts it like this: "Only of a living human being and what resembles (behaves like) a living human being can one say: it has sensations; it sees; is blind; hears; is deaf; is conscious or unconscious." [12]

I said that the conjunction, "He has no body and he thinks he is breathing," presents an "inconsistency" of a peculiar sort, arising from the fact that the two conjuncts are "at odds" with each other. This is easily seen. If the second conjunct presupposes the employment of the ordinary criteria for attributing thoughts and beliefs to others, the first conjunct cancels that presupposition. The sentence "He thinks he is breathing" is stripped, by the first conjunct, of any criteria for applying it to real situations. The first conjunct threatens the intelligibility of the second one. Our ordinary understanding of how to operate with sentences of the form "He thinks that p" is frustrated when we are invited to apply them to bodiless beings. It would seem that the conflict between the two conjuncts prevents the total conjunction from having sense.

We learn to employ many sentences of the form "He thinks that p." We know what to look for and what to do, to decide their application to situations. We learn to recognize circumstances in which a sentence of that form is a true description, and others in which it is a false description, and still other ("borderline") cases in which it is not definitely the one or the other. This *control* of the sentence is lost if it is presented to us with the condition that it is supposed to refer to a bodiless person. The criteria that we use for

12. Wittgenstein, *Philosophical Investigations*, ed. G. E. M. Anscombe and R. Rhees, trans. G. E. M. Anscombe (Oxford, 1953), para. 281.

identifying persons, and the criteria we use for determining what a person is thinking, cannot be employed under that condition.

I will draw a preliminary conclusion from these considerations. Later, I will modify it. In respect to the sentence "He has no body and he thinks he is breathing," my preliminary conclusion is that if we are supposed to be referring to some person, and are also supposing that person to have no body, then we do not know how to apply the sentence "He thinks he is breathing." And if we, the speakers of the language, would not know how to apply it under the condition laid down by the first conjunct, then it *has* no application under that condition. In other words, if we suppose the first conjunct true, we cannot suppose the second one to be either true or false or even borderline. The two conjuncts cannot be jointly true. The conjunction, taken as a whole, does not express a logical possibility.

In *Zettel* Wittgenstein remarks on how something may *look like* a proposition (*ein Satz*) and yet not be one. He gives as an illustration of this the following design for the construction of a steamroller:

The motor is in the inside of the hollow roller. The crank-shaft runs through the middle of the roller and is connected at both ends by spokes with the wall of the roller. The cylinder of the motor is fixed onto the inside of the roller. At first glance this construction looks like a machine. But it is a rigid system and the piston cannot move to and fro in the cylinder. We deprived it of all possibility of movement and did not know it.[13]

This is a good analogy for our Cartesian sentence. It looked at first as if the design for the steamroller presented the possibility of a machine that would work; but when we thought through the conditions we saw this not to be so. So, too, we see on reflection that our conjunctive sentence does not present a possibly true state of affairs, since the truth of the first conjunct would prevent the second conjunct from being either true or false. The two conjuncts,

---

13. Wittgenstein, *Zettel*, ed. G. E. M. Anscombe and G. H. von Wright, trans. G. E. M. Anscombe (Oxford, 1967), para. 248. I have departed slightly from Anscombe's translation.

added together, yield nonsense, just as the total design for the steamroller is nonsense.

It will be recalled that earlier (Section 5) I drew attention to the truth-value connection between first- and third-person statements. One aspect of this connection is that a first-person statement is true only if its third-person counterpart is true. A corollary is that if the latter cannot be true neither can its first-person mate. This provides a case against the sentence that Descartes believed to prevent a logically possible state of affairs, namely, "I have no body and I think I am breathing." It cannot be true since its third-person counterpart cannot be true.

7.   I come now to an objection that will force me to modify my preliminary conclusion. This objection starts out by reminding us that we often recognize or identify people just by their voices, not perceiving the people themselves. Why then couldn't we recognize a familiar voice that was disembodied and which expressed to us various thoughts, hopes, fears? Why couldn't there be disembodied vocal testimony?

So far this objection is not formidable. We do recognize voices; but also we often *mistake* voices: we were convinced that we heard Robinson's voice in the hallway, but the person in the hallway turned out to be Johnson. We found out whose voice it was by seeing who was in the hallway. If I heard my daughter's voice in the next room but when I entered it no one was there, I should be stunned! If there was no evidence of trickery, I suppose I should have to think it was an hallucination.

But we can imagine more puzzling cases. Suppose Robinson died and was cremated. Later a number of his friends were supping together when they heard a voice in the room speaking to them, a voice that not only sounded like Robinson's, but in addition recounted many things that no human person other than Robinson would have known. Was Robinson speaking to them! I am pretty sure that different people would have different inclinations here.

Some would say: "How could there be that voice unless it was a person speaking? And how could that person be anyone other than Robinson, since he alone knew what was recounted?" Others would say: "How could Robinson, who was *cremated*, talk to us? Surely it is more intelligible to think that the voice was *no one's* voice. Perhaps it was some remarkable meteorological phenomenon. But not even *trying* to explain it would be better than talking nonsense."

I do not see that the garland of truth could be awarded to either of these opposing viewpoints. To attribute the voice to Robinson is shocking. To say that it is no one's voice is shocking. If no further facts were to come to light, I believe that in this extraordinary situation it would not be definitely right or wrong to say that Robinson was speaking, nor would it be definitely right or wrong to say that no one was speaking. There would be those opposing inclinations; but they would be *merely* inclinations, without either being the *correct* thing to say.

Perhaps the chief value of this imaginary case is that it reminds us of a definite fact, namely, that many people have *believed* that ghosts, angels, dead relatives, saints, God and gods, have spoken to them. Consider this famous occurrence: Saul of Tarsus was traveling to Damascus when suddenly a light flashed from the sky. He fell to the ground and heard a voice say, "Saul, Saul, why do you persecute me?" Saul said, "Tell me who you are." The voice answered, "I am Jesus whom you are persecuting."

Suppose someone were to remark as follows: 'This occurrence, which had such vast consequences for the history of Christianity, may have actually been a case of mistaken identity. Perhaps the voice was not the voice of Jesus but of an imposter. Perhaps it was *just* a voice—not *anyone's* voice. Paul may have been mistaken in believing that the voice was the voice of someone, and also in believing that the someone was Jesus."

These remarks would strike me silly. Why so? Because they imply that the various devices by which persons are identified in social gatherings, police investigations, or loan offices were, or could have been, or should have been, brought into play in this incident on the road to Damascus. Instead, I suggest, we should see it as a case, not where there was a careless use of criteria of identity, but rather as one in which *no* criteria were employed. The narrative in Acts implies that Paul had unquestioning conviction; he did not seek any proof that it was Jesus who spoke to him. This is unlike the example of the disciple Thomas, who did desire a proof that it was Jesus who had visited the other disciples after the Resurrection. Thomas wanted to employ a normal test for identity—to determine by touch whether the visitor had bodily wounds matching those that Jesus had received. When Jesus appeared a second time to the disciples Thomas was convinced, although the Gospel of John does not say that he actually made the test.

The point of philosophical interest is that these two narratives from the New Testament depict two different *forms* of belief in the presence and identity of a person, the one form employing bodily criteria of identity, the other one not. Isn't it evident that cases in which people believe that they hear voices from the grave or from on high, or that they have received visitations from ghosts and spirits of the dead; or have been addressed by angelic messengers or by God Himself are cases wherein no bodily grounds of identity are employed? Not only are disembodied persons referred to, but also various thoughts and desires are attributed to them without any reliance on the criteria of bodily behavior that I emphasized in Section 6.

I can imagine a philosopher declaring that such cases should not exist, or that they are nonsensical. I would regard such an attitude as highly *un*philosophical. I agree with Wittgenstein's perception that the job of philosophy is to note and compare forms of language and thought; not to judge them to be justified or unjustified, nor to declare that this one makes sense and that one doesn't. "Philosophy may in no way interfere with the actual use of language; it can in the end only describe it." [14]

14. Wittgenstein, *Investigations*, para. 124.

8. Thus there is a domain of actual language and thought, wherein persons (including human persons) are referred to, and to whom various thoughts and feelings are attributed, without the presupposition that the persons referred to are corporeal beings. With this admission have I not surrendered to Descartes? Did I not maintain that a conjunction of the form "*x* has no body and *x* thinks that *p*" cannot present a logical possibility—that there would be a conflict between the two conjuncts which would keep the conjunction from having sense? But now I have granted that there are modes of thought and conviction, which certainly cannot be dismissed by philosophy as senseless, and wherein there occurs the attribution of present judgments, feelings, desires—to deceased friends and relatives, to spirits, invisible gods, unseen presences. In Jewish and Christian religious thought the Creator is commonly conceived of as a non-material being and yet is also conceived of as making judgments, feeling compassion, being angered. In acknowledging these systems of belief I have granted that sentences of the form "*x* has no body and *x* thinks that *p*" do make sense. How can I maintain any longer that the second premise of Descartes' deductive argument is spoiled by some sort of incoherence?

It is true that I must attach a qualification to my previous contention. In doing so I draw on Wittgenstein's distinction between a "primary" and a "secondary" *employment of a concept* (or: a primary and a secondary use of language). Wittgenstein first calls attention to this distinction in paragraph 282 of the *Investigations*, following immediately upon the remark I quoted from 281, wherein he had observed that one can say that something does or doesn't have sensations, is or isn't conscious, only if it is either a living human being or resembles (behaves like) a living human being. If this remark were taken strictly it would imply that it is senseless to attribute thoughts and desires to the Creator, or to loved ones who had perished. Yet it would be antithetical to Wittgenstein's philosophical outlook to reject as senseless any such actual "language-games."

In 282 he says: "We do say of an inanimate thing that it is in pain: when playing with dolls for example. But this use of the concept of pain is a secondary one. Imagine a case in which people ascribed pain only to inanimate things; pitied only dolls!" [15] This invitation to imagination is ironical. People who did not ascribe pain to one another or to animals would be so strange in their behavior and responses that we could not attribute to them any grasp of the concept of pain; whatever it is they are doing with dolls they are not ascribing *pain* to them. This simple example serves to explain the distinction: the secondary use of a concept can be credited to someone only if he also makes a primary use of it. The secondary use is dependent on the primary use, not the other way round.

Another example of the secondary use of concepts is the phenomenon of telling a dream. A person could not be credited with telling a dream unless he had previously acquired some ability to use language to refer to and describe physical realities. Still another secondary employment of language consists of reports and descriptions of mental images and after-images. The use of the expressions "seeing *x* in one's mind" or "hearing *y* in one's head" could be taught to a person only *after* he had learned a more primitive employment of the words "see" and "hear," in response to publicly observable objects.

The ascription of thoughts, feelings, desires, to the dead, to God and gods, to immaterial spirits, in ritual, thanksgiving, and prayer, has always been important in the life of mankind. I do not *disparage* it in regarding it as a secondary use of concepts. I do not mean that it lacks force, importance, or truth. I mean only that this employment of psychological concepts is *dependent* on an application of those concepts that is based on the human figure and countenance, and on the expressive behavior of living, bodily, human beings. The primary use of the psychological concepts could exist without the secondary one, but not vice versa.

15. The positioning of the remarks of 282 indicate that Wittgenstein wanted them to be understood as qualifying and supplementing the remark that I quoted from 281.

9.   This brings us back to Descartes. When he asserted that *I think I am breathing* does not entail *I have a body*, he did not mean that this held true only for himself. What he meant was something extremely general. He meant that the propositional form "*x* thinks that *p*" does not entail the propositional form, "*x* has a body." This implies that for *all* values of *x* (as well as for all values of *p*), a proposition of the form "*x* has no body and *x* thinks that *p*" presents a logical possibility. To state Descartes' position in even more general terms: he meant that every being whatever who has thoughts, feelings, emotions, intentions, sensations, *could* (logically speaking) have existed without a body and yet have had those same thoughts, sensations, and so on. When he said in the *Sixth Meditation*, "It is certain that this I (that is to say, my soul, by which I am what I am) is entirely and absolutely distinct from my body, and can exist without it," [16] he meant that not only himself and all other thinking, conscious beings *can* exist without bodies, but also that they *could* have existed without *ever* having had bodies. You and I, and all other human minds, could have existed in an incorporeal state throughout the entire time of our existence, yet having all the thoughts, wishes, intentions we now have. [17]

16.   HR I, 190; AT VII, 78.

17.   When I read an earlier version of the present essay at the Moral Science Club in Cambridge, some members of the audience objected that Descartes' view may have been *only* this: that having once existed in an embodied state and as a member of a linguistic community, and thus having learned a common language, he could later come to be disembodied and yet continue to think to himself in the terms of the language that he had learned to apply in conformity with the practice of that community of speakers of which he had previously been a member. Of course it is true that Descartes held that "the extinction of the mind does not follow from the corruption of the body" (*Synopsis* of the *Meditations*). But his device of "doubting" all of his former "opinions," or of "imagining" them to be false, implies more than this. In the *Second Meditation* he says: "I suppose, then, that all the things that I see are false: I persuade myself that nothing has ever existed of all that my fallacious memory represents to me. I consider that I possess no senses; I imagine that body, figure, extension, movement and place are but the fictions of my mind." These remarks surely imply that it is logically or metaphysically possible that he and his thinking should have existed even though no corporeal world had ever existed. Furthermore, Descartes states unequivocally that God *could have created him without a body*. In responding to Arnauld's criticism of the reasoning of the *Meditations* by

This position of Descartes' is, I think, a conceptual impossibility. Consider, first of all, the problem of how the thoughts, intentions, sensations could be *expressed*. There would not be the vehicle of the human figure, face, gestures, movements, to serve for this. Then would the thoughts be expressible only in language? But in *which* language? It would appear impossible that disembodied beings should have a *common* language. For what would it mean to say that they did or didn't use the terms of the language *in the same way?* Then would each of them have his own "mental" language? Now surely each private "mental" language would have to have rules—for how could there be a language without any rules? Then, would each thinker obey the rules of his own language just in his own mind? But Wittgenstein has pointed out that this makes no sense, for it would imply that *following* a rule, and *believing* one was following a rule, would come to the same—which of course they don't.[18] Finally, the problem cannot be skipped over by supposing that the thoughts of the incorporeal beings might not be expressed in language at all but might just be "naked" thoughts. For the thinking of those incorporeal minds would presumably *refer*

---

which Descartes intends to prove that nothing corporeal belongs to his nature, Descartes says: "Although perhaps there is much in me of which I have no knowledge . . . yet since that which I am aware of in myself [namely, thinking] is sufficient to allow of my existing with it as my sole possession, *I am certain that God could have created me without giving me those other things* [e.g., a body] of which I am not yet aware" (HR II, 97; AT VII, 219; emphasis added. I have departed from the Haldane-Ross translation). In addition, the passage I quote from the *Notae in Programma*, in footnote 21, makes it clear that in Descartes' view there is no dependence *whatever* between the concept of mind and the concept of body. For he says that he had "deduced and demonstrated that mind was clearly perceived by us as an existence, or substance, *even supposing we had no concept whatever of the body*, or even denied that any material things had existence; and, accordingly, that *the concept of mind does not involve any concept of body*" (emphasis added). The objection raised in Cambridge does show that there is an ambiguity in characterizing Descartes' view as being this: that he is "essentially" a non-material thing. For this could be taken as meaning merely that *after* having lived a corporeal human life he could continue to exist as a disembodied mind. In contrast, the strict and correct interpretation of his view is that he could have existed, with all his thoughts, even if he had *never* lived an embodied human life.

18. Wittgenstein, *Investigations*, para. 202.

to various things and *ascribe* properties to them. But referring and ascribing are special activities, each having a special "logic." Not just anything one does come under those headings. To speak of referring or ascribing is to invoke a system of conventions, of accepted practices. For example, *pointing* (a form of referring) rests on the convention that the direction of pointing is from shoulder to outstretched finger, not the reverse. How could there be conventions, agreed-on practices, in a total universe of incorporeal minds? How could that *mean* anything?

10.   Here it would be appropriate to comment on my strategy (in Section 5) of switching from first-person to third-person statements. Descartes would object to this maneuver; and also he would discount, as irrelevant, the remarks I made (in Section 6) about the normal criteria for applying third-person psychological sentences. Why would he do this? Because those attitudes would be consequences of the so-called "method of doubt" employed by him in the *Meditations.* In claiming that it was rational for him to doubt that he had a body, and in claiming that he could imagine that "body, figure, extension, movement and place are but the fictions of my mind" (*Second Meditation*), Descartes implied that it was a logical (or metaphysical) possibility that he should have existed as an incorporeal thinking being in an incorporeal world. He implied that had there been no Europe, earth, or any inhabited place, nor any nations, societies, or peoples, nor French, Latin, or any languages at all—that even so it would have been *logically possible* that he (his mind) should have engaged in the speculations of the *Meditations.* For my purposes, however, Descartes' most important assumption was that an incorporeal mind in an incorporeal world *could* have a full understanding of all of the psychological concepts, and could correctly attribute to itself a gamut of thoughts, sensations and emotions.

Certainly there can be a play of imagination here, just as when we imagine a conversation between a table and a chair. This is a secondary use of language. Yet the concepts employed in such imaginative play are rooted in patterns of behavior of living human beings. It was possible for Descartes to believe otherwise *because* of the fact that a person does not, for the most part, ascribe feelings, thoughts, sensations, to himslef *on the basis of observing his own behavior*. But Wittgenstein says something that goes to the heart of this matter:

> We do not say that *possibly* a dog talks to itself. Is that because we are so minutely acquainted with its soul? Well, one might say this: If one sees the behavior of a living thing, one sees its soul.—But do I also say in my own case that I am saying something to myself, because I am behaving in such-and-such a way?—I do *not* say it from observation of my behavior. *But it only makes sense because I do behave in this way.*[19]

To what sort of behavior might Wittgenstein have been referring? Well, suppose that what I said to myself was "I refuse to grant his request." It would make sense to credit me with declaring this to myself only if I had learned, for instance, the concept of *refusing*, a concept that ranges over a great variety of circumstances and actions—for example, my thrusting away with my hand something that was offered me. My declaring, whether to myself or to others, that I "refuse" such and such would not make sense if my previous employment of that word had never been linked with the right behavior.

11.   Let us see where we are. In studying Descartes' proof I concentrated on his second premise. I employed the strategy of examining its third-person counterpart. The initial justification for this was that a first- and third-person pair must have the same truth-value; consequently, if a third-person sentence lacks sense so must its first-person mate. I noticed an odd sort of conflict between the use of the sentences "He has no body" and "He thinks he is breathing." This conflict, although it can be loosely called an "inconsistency," does not seem to be a *contradiction* in any strict sense. If this is so, then it is true that "He thinks that p" does not *entail* "He has a body." Furthermore, it is an ordinary use of language to attri-

19. Ibid., para. 357. My emphasis added to the final sentence.

bute thoughts, desires, feelings, to beings conceived to be incorporeal, even though this must be regarded as a secondary employment of concepts. Switching to the third person helped, however, to remind us of how behavioral criteria govern the application of third-person psychological sentences. It also brought in Wittgenstein's insight that although my affirming that I think or feel such and such does not arise from my applying behavioral criteria to myself, nevertheless my affirming this *makes sense* only because I do largely satisfy those criteria. Descartes failed to see that the meaning of first-person psychological attributions is dependent on the existence and behavior of living, corporeal human beings.

12.   What is the upshot in regard to Descartes' contention that *I think I am breathing* does not entail *I have a body?* It seems to me that this question must be treated at two different levels. At one level we have to agree that there is no entailment. It does not appear that there could be a substitution of terms, in accordance with any plausible definitions, that would establish a *formal* inconsistency between the sentences "I think I am breathing" and "I have no body." Someone might try to achieve this by the device of asserting an identity of reference between "I" and "my body." But the assertion "I am identical with my body" would be tendentious; and furthermore, it does not seem to me to have any clear meaning. How would one undertake to verify it? All in all, there is no natural, uncontroversial, sense in which the conjunction of the two sentences "I think I am breathing" and, "I have no body" can be exhibited as self-contradictory. Considered in this light, "I think I am breathing" does not entail "I have a body," anymore than it entails "I have a sunburn."

Thus there is a level at which Descartes' argument can be rightly deemed to be both valid and sound. If we waive any doubts about the meaningfulness of "I exist," as employed in the context of Descartes' soliloquy, and if we admit, as I think we must, that "I have a body" cannot be deduced from "I think I am breathing," and if we ignore a reservation to be made in Section 14, then we must agree that Descartes hit upon a valid argument with true premises, namely:

> *I think I am breathing* entails *I exist.*
> *I think I am breathing* does not entail *I have a body.*
> Therefore, *I exist* does not entail *I have a body.*

As said before, this conclusion is equivalent to: *It is logically possible that I should exist without a body.* As I have pointed out (see footnote 17), this had to be taken as meaning not just that it is possible that, having once had a bodily existence, I could *continue* to exist without a body. It must be taken as meaning this: *It is logically possible that I should have existed without ever having had a body.*

But now we need to ask: Who is this *I* to whom Descartes is referring? It cannot be *Descartes.* Descartes is a historical person who was born of certain parents, who lived in France and Holland in the seventeenth century, served in a military campaign, made mathematical discoveries, wrote various philosophical works, corresponded with Father Mersenne, and so on, and so on. Anyone of whom no such historical facts were true would not be *Descartes.* Therefore, we cannot consider Descartes to have proved that it is logically possible that *Descartes* should have existed without ever having had a body.

Of course any person whomsoever could pronounce the sentences of Descartes' argument. I could, for example. But to whom would I be referring? Not to *Malcolm.* Malcolm is a human being who was born of certain parents in the Middle West of the USA in the twentieth century, who delivered newspapers, was caused to have appendicitis by a horse, became a Doctor of Philosophy, wrote an infamous book entitled *Dreaming*, and so on, and so on. Anyone of whom none of those historical facts were true would not be *Malcolm.*

It is worth noting that Descartes, from his own standpoint, could not have been talking about *Descartes.* His general doubt, which led up to the *cogito*, included a doubt as to whether there had ever been a material world, and therefore included a doubt as to whether there had ever existed the historical person *Descartes*. G. E. M. Anscombe calls attention to this in a recent essay. Speaking of Descartes' argument to prove that *this I* is not a body, she says:

Whatever else is said, it seems clear that the argument in Descartes depends on results of applying the method of doubt. But by that method Descartes must have doubted the existence of the man Descartes: at any rate of that figure in the world of his time, that Frenchman, born of such-and-such a stock and christened René; but also, even of the man—unless a man isn't a sort of animal. *If*, then, the non-identity of himself with his own body follows from his starting-points, so equally does the non-identity of himself with the man Descartes. "I am not Descartes" was just as sound a conclusion for him to draw as "I am not a body." . . . That which is named by "I"—*that*, in *his* book, was not *Descartes*.[20]

In regard to the valid argument of Descartes' that is the topic of the present essay, I think we must say the following: That even if we take it to be a *sound* argument (i.e., as having true premises, as well as being valid) it does not serve as a proof that Descartes, or any other human person, is essentially a non-material thing. One thing that makes it a peculiar and puzzling argument is that the reference of the word "I" is totally unclear.

Undoubtedly Descartes' argument is an interesting logical discovery. But we should not misinterpret the import of it, as did Descartes. It is unreasonable to expect that the complex ways in which our use of the mental concepts is influenced by the human bodily form and behavior should be made manifest at the level of logical entailment. Descartes' argument will not yield the dramatic metaphysical consequence he thought he had achieved. It is tempting to accept, unwittingly, the superficial grammar of his argument as a proof of the metaphysical thesis that in 1647 Descartes stated as follows: "The concept of mind does not involve any concept of body."[21] If we read the second premise of Descartes' argument in

20. G. E. M. Anscombe, "The First Person," *Mind and Language*, ed. S. Guttenplan, pp. 45–46.

21. The whole sentence (from the *Notae in Programma*) contains an excellent formulation of the argument from doubt: "I wrote that we could not doubt that our

the way that this metaphysical thesis requires, then it should be evident that the second premise is unacceptable. When we interpret it as the contention that our concepts of thinking and of thought could have been understood and applied, even if there had never been any living, corporeal, human beings, then nothing could be more absurd. Taken in this light, whether we call the second premise false, or nonsensical, does not matter. We are entitled to reject it, since it implies something that is really unintelligible; and this disposes of Descartes' only valid argument to prove that he is essentially a non-material thing.

13. I wish to register here an uneasiness about the expression, "logical possibility." Can something be a logical possibility if it is a conceptual impossibility? Apparently so. If we take "entailment" as meaning that p entails q (where the range of the variables "p" and "q" is restricted to contingent propositions) if and only if the conjunction, p and *not-q*, is self-contradictory; and if, accordingly, we say that when this conjunction is not self-contradictory p does *not* entail q; and if we formulate this latter state of affairs in the terminology of "logical possibility," saying that it is a logical possibility that p and *not-q* should both be true at the same time; then it seems we are forced to agree with Descartes that it is a logical possibility that, at one and the same time, I should think I am breathing and yet should have no body. (There is a problem, however, as to whether "I have no body" is a meaningful proposition, which I shall take up in a moment.)

Well, this is all right as far as it goes; but it doesn't go very far. It certainly does not yield the metaphysical thesis that the mental concepts, in their actual use, are entirely separated from consider-

---

mind existed, because, from the very fact that we doubted, it followed that our mind existed, but that meantime we might doubt whether any material thing existed; whence I deduced and demonstrated that mind was clearly perceived by us as an existence, or substance, even supposing we had no concept whatever of the body, or even denied that any material things had existence; and, accordingly, that the concept of mind does not involve any concept of body" (HR I, 440; AT VIII, 354. I have deviated slightly from the Haldane-Ross translation).

ations of the bodily figure and behavior of human beings. It seems to me that the expression "logical possibility" as used here, can be dangerously confusing. There is no objection to it when it is taken strictly in a narrow sense, as expressing the absence of entailment. But we are inevitably tempted to give it a *deeper* meaning. I would myself prefer to limit the deeper meaning to the expression "conceptual possibility." This is no cure for anything; yet this latter expression is less misleading, I think, in the respect that it suggests to us that we should study the actual use of concepts, rather than confining our attention to the question of whether a combination of two sentences is self-contradictory.

14. In my examination of Descartes' argument I have focused on the claim, implied by the second premise, that the conjunction, "I have no body and I think I am breathing," expresses a logical possibility. I have contended that this conjunction involves a peculiar sort of "inconsistency," an inconsistency that is brought into the open by reflection on the third-person counterpart of that conjunction. But now I want to say something about the first conjunct of Descartes' conjunction, namely, "I have no body." In the discussion at Cambridge Mary Geach pointed out that there would be an absurdity in the statement "I have no body." I could be in a condition in which I could neither see, touch, or feel any part of my body, nor would have any kinaesthetic, muscular, or other bodily sensations. Let us call this a condition of "sensory deprivation." But how could I move from my awareness of being in a state of sensory deprivation to the conclusion that I have no body? Certainly, I could not verify the latter by sense-perception, nor by overhearing the testimony of others; for in either case I would be assuming some normal functioning of my sensory organs. It appears that the statement "I have no body" would be unverifiable for conceptual reasons. There would be a kind of nonsense in my asserting or inferring that *I have no body*, which is very similar (as Miss Geach remarked) to the kind of nonsense involved in my asserting or inferring that *I am asleep*. This is a further reason for

holding that Descartes' conjunction does not express a conceptual possibility. Not only is there an inconsistency, of a conceptual sort, between the two parts of the conjunction but, in addition, the first member of the conjunction is a conceptual absurdity, when taken as a statement in its own right.

15.   As a final note, I will mention a curiosity. An argument can be constructed, which is of the same valid form as Descartes' argument, yet leads to a conclusion unacceptable to him. Consider the following reasoning:

> *I am breathing* entails *I exist.*
> *I am breathing* does not entail *I am thinking.*
> Therefore, *I exist* does not entail *I am thinking.*

Now Descartes held that I am essentially a thinking being, and he understood this as meaning that at no moment of my existence could I fail to be thinking. In a letter to Hyperaspistes in 1641 he said:

I had reason to assert that the human soul, wherever it be, even in the mother's womb, is always thinking. What more certain or evident reason could be wished for than the one I gave? I had proved that the nature or essence of soul consists in the fact that it is thinking, just as the essence of body consists in the fact that it is extended. Now nothing can ever be deprived of its own essence; so it seems to me that a man who denies that his soul was thinking at times when he does not remember noticing it thinking, deserves no more attention than a man who denied that his body was extended while he did not notice that it had extension.[22]

The conclusion of the deductive argument I have just put together implies that it is logically possible that I should exist and not be thinking. It is hard to see how Descartes could reject either of the premises. Surely he ought to accept the first premise. And how could he object to the second premise, except by begging the question in favor of his thesis that my essential nature is to think? Thus we have the irony that the same form of valid deductive argument

22. Kenny, *Letters*, 111; AT III, 423.

that Descartes employed as a proof of his thesis that he is essentially a non-material thing can be used to prove the profoundly anti-Cartesian thesis that he is *not* a being whose essential nature is thinking.

4 | *Behaviorism as a Philosophy of Psychology*

As a philosopher I have a professional reluctance to make observations about an empirical science and especially so in the presence of some of its distinguished practitioners. I am emboldened by the belief that the dispute over the place of behaviorism in psychology is fundamentally a philosophical issue. In saying this I do not imply that it is an issue which cannot be resolved and with respect to which we must content ourselves with opinions or attitudes. On the contrary, I think that what is right and wrong with the viewpoint and assumptions of behaviorism can be clearly formulated.

A FAILURE TO DISAGREE

Professor Rogers claims that behaviorism has had an unfortunate effect on psychology. It impoverishes psychology by excluding from its data the "private worlds" of people, the "flow of their inner experience," "the whole universe of inner meanings," the purposes, goals, values, and choices of people, and their "perceptions of self." He calls all of this "the phenomenal world of the individual," [1] and he says that "Not one aspect of this world is open to the strict behaviorist." [2] He believes that psychology needs to be

This essay was presented in a colloquium, at Rice University, to which Professors Rogers and Skinner were contributors.

1. C. R. Rogers, "Toward a Science of the Person," *Behaviorism and Phenomenology: Contrasting Bases for Modern Psychology*, ed. T. W. Wann (Chicago, 1964), p. 119.

2. Ibid.

enriched by "a science of the inner life" that will attempt to find lawful relationships between these phenomena and "external behavior." A study which concerns itself with these "inner variables" must be added to empirical psychology if this science is to obtain any deep understanding of human life.

I am willing to bet (a small sum) that Professor Skinner finds this criticism puzzling, because he cannot see in it any specific theoretical issue that divides him and Rogers. Whether Skinner is puzzled or not, I am. I do not see that Skinner's behaviorism commits him to denying or ignoring the existence of the "inner variables" which Rogers thinks are so important. Let me explain.

Skinner is an exponent of a "functional analysis" of human behavior. He holds that every piece of human behavior is a "function" of some condition that is describable in physical terms, as is the behavior itself.[3] The conditions of which behavior is a function are, for the most part, external to the organism, although sometimes they may be "within the organism's skin."[4] The physical conditions of which behavior is a function are called "independent variables," and the pieces of behavior are the "dependent variables." A dependent variable is said to be under the "control" of an independent variable. The relations between independent and dependent variables are scientific laws. The aim of behavioristic psychology is to uncover these laws, thus making possible the prediction and control of human behavior. "A synthesis of these laws expressed in quantitative terms yields a comprehensive picture of the organism as a behaving system."[5]

Skinner devotes considerable attention to what he calls "explanatory fictions." Some of his examples are being *thirsty*, or *hungry*,[6] being *absent-minded* or having *confused ideas*,[7] being *interested* or *discouraged* or having a *sense of achievement*,[8] having an *incentive* or *goal* or *purpose*,[9] and the *intent* behind an action or the *meaning* of it.[10]

3. B. F. Skinner, *Science and Human Behavior* (New York, 1953), pp. 35, 36.
4. Ibid., p. 257.   5. Ibid., p. 35.   6. Ibid., p. 31.
7. Ibid., p. 30.   8. Ibid., p. 72.   9. Ibid., pp. 87–88.
10. Ibid., p. 36.

All of these are examples of what some philosophers call "psychological" or "mental" concepts. I think that anything any philosopher would want to call a "psychological" concept Skinner would consider to be an explanatory fiction. In saying that they are explanatory fictions Skinner means that they are *not* explanatory. Take such an apparent explanation as "He is drinking because he is thirsty." Skinner says: "If to be thirsty means nothing more than to have a tendency to drink, this is mere redundancy. If it means that he drinks because of a state of thirst, an inner causal event is invoked. If this state is purely inferential—if no dimensions are assigned to it which would make direct observation possible—it cannot serve as an explanation." [11] When you speak of a man's "purpose" in doing something or say that he has stopped doing something because he is "discouraged," you are not saying anything worth saying unless you are making a reference, perhaps concealed, to the independent variables which control his behavior. [12]

Skinner's remarks about explanatory fictions are sometimes slightly ambiguous. Sometimes he seems to be saying that there really is not any such thing as, for example, *a sense of achievement*. "We do not give a man a sense of achievement," he says, "we reinforce a particular action." [13] When a man is said to be "looking for something," "There is no *current* goal, incentive, purpose, or meaning to be taken into account." [14] This would seem to be a denial that the man really has a purpose in doing what he does. But I do not believe that Skinner wants to be in the absurd position of really denying that people are sometimes encouraged or discouraged or that they have goals and purposes, any more than he wants to deny that they get thirsty. Instead, he is trying to say how these terms are to be understood. Such terms as "meaning" and "intent," he says, "usually conceal references to independent variables." [15] "Statements which use such words as 'incentive' or 'purpose' are usually reducible to statements about operant conditioning." [16] Skinner will agree that people have purposes, but holds that mean-

11. Ibid., p. 33.   12. Ibid., e.g., pp. 36, 72.   13. Ibid., p. 72.
14. Ibid., pp. 89–90.   15. Ibid., p. 36.   16. Ibid., p. 87.

ingful statements about purposes are reducible to statements about functional relations between independent and dependent variables.

Let us come back to Rogers' criticism of Skinner. The purposes, goals, values, and choices of people, their "private worlds," their "perceptions of self," their "inner experience"—all of those phenomena which, according to Rogers, behaviorism cannot deal with, are examples of Skinner's explanatory fictions. Skinner would willingly accept them as significant phenomena insofar as they can be handled by functional analysis. If you can define them in terms of functional relations between external or internal physical variables and the observable behavior of people, then well and good. If not, then it is not clear what you are talking about.

What I find puzzling is that Rogers himself seems to admit this or at least to go halfway toward admitting it. He allows that the study of the "inner variables" of which he speaks—"requires careful definition of observable behaviors which are indexes of these subjective variables. It is recognized that variables of inner experience cannot be measured directly, but it is also realized that the fact that they *are* inner variables does not preclude their scientific study." [17] He foresees the development of "operational steps" for the "measurement of the behaviors which represent these inner variables." [18] Skinner could retort that the observable behavior and physical conditions, which are said by Rogers to "represent" the inner variables, either do or do not define them. If they do, then the "inner" has become "outer," and functional analysis can go full steam ahead. If not, then the expressions which allegedly "represent" inner variables have not been given any meaning.

My conclusion is that Rogers has not shown some theoretical flaw in behaviorism. Skinner could hold that Rogers' "science of the person" would fall, insofar as it has an intelligible subject matter, within the wider domain of functional analysis of behavior. It would be one branch or division of behavioristic science and not an alternative or addition to it.

17. Rogers, p. 130.   18. Ibid., p. 131.

THE PHILOSOPHICAL BASIS OF BEHAVIORISM

Behaviorism, in my view, is essentially a *philosophical* doctrine. Skinner is agreeing with this when he says that behaviorism is "a philosophy of science concerned with the subject matter and methods of psychology." [19] Behaviorism, as a philosophy of psychology, is continuous with the philosophical doctrine of *physicalism*, which was expounded by Rudolf Carnap and other members of the so-called Vienna Circle. I will set forth some of Carnap's views on this topic in order to bring out the close resemblance between Carnap's physicalism and Skinner's behaviorism.

The basic thesis of physicalism, according to Carnap, is that "every sentence of psychology may be formulated in physical language." [20] When put in "the material mode of speech," the thesis is that "all sentences of psychology describe physical occurrences, namely, the physical behavior of humans and other animals." [21] Carnap says, "Our thesis thus states that a definition may be constructed for every psychological concept (i.e., expression) which directly or indirectly derives that concept from physical concepts." [22] Psychological laws, too, are translatable into physical language (i.e., into language which describes physical conditions and occurrences), and therefore they are a subclass of physical laws. [23]

The pure philosophical principle behind this thesis is the so-called Verification Principle: "The meaning of a statement is its method of verification." As Carnap puts it, "A sentence says no more than what is testable about it." [24] Thus a statement that I make about another person, e.g., that he is excited or angry, can mean nothing else than that he is behaving in such and such a way, that he will respond in such and such a way to certain stimuli, that his central nervous system is in such and such a state, and so on. [25] If we try to claim that over and above, or behind, these physical

19. Skinner, "Behaviorism at Fifty," *Behaviorism and Phenomenology*, p. 79.
20. R. Carnap, "Psychology in Physical Language," *Erkenntnis*, 3 (1932–33). reprinted in *Logical Positivism*, ed. A. J. Ayer (Glencoe, Ill., 1959), p. 165.
21. Ibid.   22. Ibid., p. 167.   23. Ibid.   24. Ibid., p. 174.
25. Ibid., e.g., p. 172.

facts there is an inner state of excitement or anger, which is entirely different from the actual and/or potential behavior and the physiological state, and which might or might not be present with these physical facts, then we are claiming something that we do not know how to verify. Our assertion that this person is angry turns out to be "a metaphysical pseudo-sentence." [26] It might be objected that the person could *tell* us that he felt angry, and if he was a generally truthful person we should have evidence for the existence of an inner state of anger. Carnap's reply is that the person's statement does not inform us of anything unless we *understand* it, and we do not understand it unless we know what observable phenomena would verify it. As Carnap puts it, "If the sentence 'A was angry yesterday at noon' has no meaning for me—as would be the case if . . . I could not test it—it will not be rendered meaningful by the fact that a sound having the structure of this sentence came from A's own mouth." [27] The fact that we rely on the testimony of people as a source of information about them does not relieve us of the necessity of giving a physical interpretation of the sentences they utter, an interpretation which will make those sentences testable. In Carnap's view the psychological concepts of ordinary language are a source of confusion because their reference to physical conditions and behavior is not sufficiently explicit. The clarification of these concepts will consist in "physicalising" them, i.e., in providing explicit behavioristic definitions of them. But, as Carnap says, "psychology is a physical science even prior to such a clarification of its concepts—a physical science whose assignment it is to describe systematically the (physical) behavior of living creatures, especially that of human beings, and to develop laws under which this behavior may be subsumed." [28]

There is one important respect in which Skinner's behaviorism differs from the physicalism of the Vienna Circle. The question arises as to whether the physicalizing of psychological concepts is to be in terms of the inner physiology of the human organism or in

26. Ibid., p. 174.   27. Ibid., p. 180.   28. Ibid., p. 189.

terms of its outward behavior. Carnap discusses the example of a sentence which says that a certain person is *excited*. He holds that this sentence has the same "content" as another sentence which asserts that the person's "central nervous system" is in a certain state and also that the person is making "agitated movements," or would make them on the application of certain stimuli.[29] His sample analysis of a psychological sentence refers, therefore, *both* to inner physiology and to outward behavior. This mixed reference is even more explicit in some remarks made by Carl Hempel, also a former exponent of physicalism. Discussing the psychological sentence "Paul has a toothache," Hempel asks "What is the specific content of this proposition, that is to say, what are the circumstances in which it would be verified?" He goes on to say that the following are some of the test sentences which describe these circumstances:

a) "Paul weeps and makes gestures of such and such kinds."
b) "At the question, 'What is the matter?' Paul utters the words 'I have a toothache.' "
c) "Closer examination reveals a decayed tooth with exposed pulp."
d) "Paul's blood pressure, digestive processes, the speed of his reactions, show such and such changes."
e) "Such and such processes occur in Paul's central nervous system."

Hempel declares that the proposition about Paul's pain is "simply an abbreviated expression of the fact that all its test sentences are verified." [30] It is evident that the alleged "content" of the sentence about Paul is a very mixed bag, containing references to both the outward behavior of weeping, gestures, and utterance, and also to such physiological phenomena as blood pressure, digestive processes, and events in the central nervous system.[31]

Skinner is dissatisfied, rightly I think, with physiological analy-

29. Ibid., p. 172.
30. C. G. Hempel, "The Logical Analysis of Psychology," *Readings in Philosophical Analysis*, ed. H. Feigl and W. Sellars (New York, 1949), p. 377.
31. It should be noted that both Carnap and Hempel subsequently abandoned the view that the "cognitive meaning" of an empirical statement is equivalent to all or some of its test sentences. See Hempel's "The Empiricist Criterion of Meaning," in *Logical Positivism*.

ses of psychological concepts. For one thing, he says, not enough is known about neural states and events for them to be useful in the prediction and control of specific behavior.[32] For another thing, he has a "methodological" objection. He believes that holding that the events observed or inferred in an analysis of behavior are basically physiological "does not solve the methodological problems with which behaviorism is most seriously concerned.[33] Skinner means, I believe, that behaviorism as a philosophy of psychology is trying to solve a problem that he calls "methodological" and that I should call "philosophical." The problem is, as he puts it, "how one knows about the subjective world of another."[34] Now the fact is that we know a great deal about the "subjective worlds" of others. (Here I am formulating a line of thought that I hope Skinner finds acceptable.) That is to say, we know on a great many occasions in ordinary life when someone is *angry*, *tired*, *excited*, or *perplexed*. This common knowledge we have of the mental states of others certainly is not a knowledge of physiological processes, about which we are largely ignorant. It is Skinner's view that if behaviorism is to clarify the "testable content" of psychological concepts, it should not concentrate on the inner physiology of the human organism but rather on what lies open to observation, namely, physical circumstances and outward behavior.

Skinner says: "The practice of looking inside the organism for an explanation of behavior has tended to obscure the variables which are immediately available for a scientific analysis. These variables lie outside the organism, in its immediate environment and in its environmental history."[35]

Carnap asserted: "A sentence about other minds refers to physical processes in the body of the person in question. On any other interpretation the sentence becomes untestable in principle, and thus meaningless."[36] Skinner could say, and I should agree with him, that this is a non sequitur. If the statement that a certain per-

---

32. Skinner, *Science and Human Behavior*, pp. 28–29.
33. Skinner, "Behaviorism at Fifty," p. 95.   34. Ibid., p. 83.
35. Skinner, *Science and Human Behavior*, p. 31.   36. Carnap, p. 191.

son is *discouraged* about something refers to his behavior and also to external circumstances which "control" that behavior, then the statement is testable; and it is far more readily testable than if it referred to processes in his body. Thus Skinner's brand of behaviorism explain psychological concepts in terms of outward behavior and circumstances rather than inner physiology.

Despite Skinner's justified dislike of physicalism's predilection for physiology, the basic aim of his functional analysis is the same as that of physicalism, namely, to achieve a clarification of psychological concepts which will make it evident that psychology is truly a physical science. Like the philosophers of the Vienna Circle, he is attempting to reduce mental concepts to physical concepts, although he has a clearer idea of the form this reduction must take. It may be surprising to some to think of Skinner as engaged in a typically philosophical undertaking of reducing concepts of one kind to concepts of another kind, and therefore I will substantiate this claim by quoting from Skinner. Speaking of occupational therapy he says:

It is of no advantage to say that such therapy helps the patient by giving him a "sense of achievement" or improves his "morale," builds up his "interest," or removes or prevents "discouragement." Such terms as these merely add to the growing population of explanatory fictions. One who readily engages in a given activity is not showing an interest, he is showing the effect of reinforcement. We do not give a man a sense of achievement, we reinforce a particular action. To become discouraged is simply to fail to respond because reinforcement has not been forthcoming.[37]

Skinner remarks that it is a "fundamental principle of science" to rule out "final causes." He goes on to say:

But this principle is violated when it is asserted that behavior is under the control of an "incentive" or "goal" which the organism has not yet achieved or a "purpose" which it has not yet fulfilled. Statements which use such words as "incentive" or "purpose" are usually reducible to statements about operant conditioning, and only a slight change is required to bring them within the framework of a natural science. Instead of saying that a

37. Skinner, *Science and Human Behavior*, p. 72.

man behaves because of the consequences which *are* to follow his behavior, we simply say that he behaves because of the consequences which *have* followed similar behavior in the past.[38]

It is fairly evident that in these passages Skinner is trying to give logical analyses, i.e., reductions, of various expressions that, on his view, mislead us. He is trying to tell us what becoming discouraged *is*, what being interested *is*, and what it *is* to do something for a purpose. He pays particular attention to the notion of *looking for something*, which describes an activity in terms of its purpose. He makes this assertion: "In general, looking for something consists of emitting responses which in the past have produced 'something' as a consequence." [39] Here he is trying to tell us of what looking for something *consists*. He offers several "translations" of the sentence "I am looking for my glasses." He says that this sentence is "equivalent" to the following: " 'I have lost my glasses,' 'I shall stop what I am doing when I find my glasses,' or 'When I have done this in the past, I have found my glasses.' " He remarks that these "translations" seem "roundabout," but this is because "expressions involving goals and purposes" are "abbreviations." [40]

The remarks I have quoted make quite evident Skinner's role as a philosopher engaged in translating and reducing the misleading mentalistic expressions of ordinary language. These expressions have a disguised meaning. They are "abbreviations." Skinner's task is to unpack these abbreviations by making explicit the behavioristic variables to which they refer in a "concealed" way and which give them whatever intelligibility and usefulness they have.

I think it is easy to see what makes behaviorism attractive as a philosophy of psychology. It may be conceived of as a reaction against another philosophy of psychology (which I shall call "introspectionism"), the basic assumption of which is that each of us learns from his own case what pain, anger, fear, purpose, and so on *are*. Each of us first of all takes note of, and identifies, his own inner experiences and then surmises or infers that others have the

38. Ibid., p. 87.   39. Ibid., p. 89.   40. Ibid., p. 90.

same inner experiences. I believe that Wittgenstein has proved this line of thinking to be disastrous.[41] It leads to the conclusion that we do not and cannot understand each other's psychological language, which is a form of solipsism. Worse than this (if that is possible), it leads to the result that one's identification of one's own inner experience might be wrong without one's ever being the wiser. Not only might it be the case that what I identify in myself as "anger" is not what others identify in themselves as "anger," but also it might be that what I identify in myself as "anger" is a *different* something each time, although I *think* it is the same. If it were something different each time then I should not be identifying anything. Whether this were so or not could not be determined, either by myself or anyone else. Introspectionism assumes that each of us makes *correct* identifications of his mental states. But if it makes no sense to determine that my identification is right or wrong, then it does not *have* a right or wrong, and therefore it is not an identification of anything. Introspectionism is a self-refuting doctrine, because its assumption that each of us obtains his mastery of psychological concepts from introspection actually leads to the collapse of the notion of inner identification.

One does not have to accept the Verification Principle "whole hog" in order to acknowledge the strong point of behaviorism. The refutation of introspectionism, on purely philosophical grounds, proves that our concepts of mental states and events cannot be divorced from human behavior. As we noted previously, this problem cannot be avoided by the maneuver of holding that *verbal* behavior is a sufficient foundation for our common psychological concepts. Skinner is keenly aware of this point. He says, "We cannot avoid the responsibility of showing how a private event can ever come to be described by the individual or, in the same sense, be known to him." [42] Skinner puts the point with equal sharpness in his paper for the present colloquium. He talks about a case in which some students applied various psychological terms to the be-

41. Wittgenstein, *Philosophical Investigations*.
42. Skinner, *Science and Human Behavior*, p. 280.

havior of a pigeon. They said, for example, that the pigeon *hoped* for food, *expected* reinforcement, and so on. Skinner is willing to say that the students were reporting what they themselves "would have expected, felt, and hoped for under similar circumstances." [43] But he goes on to emphasize that they must have learned these terms from a "verbal community" which *"had access only to the kinds of public information available to the students in the demonstration.* Whatever the students knew about themselves which permitted them to infer comparable events in the pigeon must have been learned from a verbal community which saw no more of their behavior than they had seen of the pigeon's." [44] I believe that Skinner has stated here an absolutely decisive objection to introspectionism. The intelligibility of psychological words must be based on something other than the occurrence of those words. That we have a common understanding of them proves that their use has to be logically connected with other public behavior.

THE FALLACY OF BEHAVIORISM

I have been trying to give an account of the hard core of logical truth contained in behaviorism, which gives it toughness as a philosophy of psychology. But now I want to disagree with behaviorism. The Achilles' heel of this doctrine lies in its treatment of psychological sentences in the first-person present tense. The same error occurs in physicalism. Let me begin to explain this by considering Carnap's sample sentence, "I am now excited." Carnap says that the "rational support" for this sentence lies in such sentences as "I feel my hands trembling," "I see my hands trembling," "I hear my voice quavering," and so on. He goes on to remark that the sentence "I am now excited" has the "same content" as the "physical" sentence "My body is now in that condition which, both under my own observation and that of others, exhibits such and such characteristics of excitement." [45] Carnap is obviously assuming that when a person says, "I am excited," his saying it is based,

43. Skinner, "Behaviorism at Fifty," p. 91.   44. Ibid.
45. Carnap, p. 191.

in part at least, on his observations of the state of his own body. The truth is that it would be a rare case in which a person said that he was excited on the basis of noticing that his hands were trembling or his voice quavering. I do not say that it is impossible for such a case to occur. A man who had narrowly escaped some danger might notice afterwards, perhaps with surprise, that his hands were trembling, and he might conclude that he must be very excited. In the normal case, however, a man does not *conclude* that he is excited. He says that he is, and he is; but his utterance is not the result of self-observation.

The point comes out very strikingly when we consider first-person reports of bodily sensations, e.g., "I have a headache." It would be completely mad if I were to say this on the basis of noticing that my face was flushed, my eyes dull, that I was holding my head, and had just taken some aspirin. If someone were to say, *on that basis*, that he has a headache, either he would be joking or else he would not understand how the words are used. The same is true of a first-person perception sentence, such as "I see a black dog." On the basis of observing that another person's eyes are following a black dog, *I* can say, "He sees a black dog." But it would make no sense for *him* to say, on the basis of noticing that his own eyes were following a black dog, that he sees a black dog.

The natural temptation to which behaviorist philosophers have succumbed is to assume that first-person psychological sentences have the same "content," or the same verification, as the corresponding third-person sentences. It looks as if that must be how it is: nevertheless, that is not how it is. I can verify that another man is excited, by the trembling of his hands. But I do not verify in this way that *I* am excited. In the normal case I do not verify it at all. By observing you I can verify that you have a headache. I do not verify that *I* have a headache. I can verify that the animal in the field is a brown cow. I cannot verify, in addition, that I *see* a brown cow. In the case of another person I can verify both that there is a brown cow in the field and that he sees it.

The notion of verification does not apply to a wide range of first-person psychological reports and utterances. Another way to put the point is to say that those reports and utterances are *not based on observations*. The error of introspectionism is to suppose that they are based on observations of inner mental events. The error of behaviorism is to suppose that they are based on observations of outward events or of physical events inside the speaker's skin. These two philosophies of psychology share a false assumption, namely, that a first-person psychological statement is a report of something the speaker has, or thinks he has, observed.

The mistake of assimilating first-person to third-person psychological statements is quite obvious in Skinner's thinking. He refers to an imaginary case in which we ask a man why he is going down the street and we receive the reply "I am going to mail a letter." Skinner says:

We have not learned anything new about his behavior but only about some of its possible causes. The subject himself, of course, may be in an advantageous position in describing these variables because he has had an extended contact with his own behavior for many years. But his statement is not therefore in a different class from similar statements made by others who have observed his behavior upon fewer occasions. . . . he is simply making a plausible prediction in terms of his experience with himself.[46]

The truth is that normally when a man tells you his purpose in doing something his statement is in a different class from a statement made by somebody else on the basis of observation of him. If you see someone rummaging about in the papers on his desk, and remember that when he had done this on previous occasions the rummaging had come to an end when he grabbed hold of his spectacles, you might reasonably conclude on these grounds that he is now looking for his spectacles. But it would be weird if *he* were to reason as follows: "Here I am rummaging about on my desk. When I have done this in the past my activity has terminated when I have caught hold of my spectacles. Therefore, I am probably looking for my spectacles"! If you heard a man make such a remark and be-

46. Skinner, *Science and Human Behavior*, p. 88.

lieved that he was not joking, you would thereafter regard him with suspicion, because of the craziness of the remark.

Skinner is puzzled by such utterances as "I was about to go home," "I am inclined to go home," "I shall go home in half an hour." He says that they "describe states of affairs which appear to be accessible only to the speaker. How can the verbal community establish responses of this sort?" He thinks a possible explanation is that when the language is learned while the individual is "behaving publicly," "private stimuli" come to be associated with the "public manifestations." The rest of this possible explanation is as follows: "Later when these private stimuli occur alone, the individual may respond to them. 'I was on the point of going home' may be regarded as the equivalent of 'I observed events in myself which characteristically precede or accompany my going home.' What these events are, such an explanation does not say." [47] For Skinner "private stimuli" would mean, of course, physical events within the individual's skin. The fact that Skinner regards this hypothesis as a possible explanation of the utterances, even though he does not know what the private stimuli would be, shows how unquestioningly he assumes that such a remark as "I am on the point of going home" must be based on the observation of something.

Undoubtedly people sometimes decide to go home because of physical disturbances within their skins. But it is wrong to suppose that the announcement "I am about to go home" is a prediction based on observation. Normally it would be outlandish to ask a man what the observational data are on the basis of which he is predicting that he is about to go home. The announcement "I am about to go home" is normally an announcement of intention. Announcements of intention are not based on the observation of either internal or external variables, despite Skinner's assumption that they must be.

Skinner would reply that surely the announcement or the intention is under the *control* of some variable. Perhaps so, depending on

47. Ibid., p. 262.

how ambiguously we use the word "control." Normally a man would have some reason for going home, e.g., that it is supper time. We might express this in some cases by saying that the fact it was supper time "determined his decision" to go home, or was the "controlling factor," or some such thing. We usually expect there will be something which controls a man's intention, in this sense. But if we mean "control" in Skinner's technical sense, according to which *y* is under the control of *x* if and only if *x* and *y* are connected by some *functional relationship*, i.e., by a *law*—if this is what we mean, then I will say that we have no ground at all for believing that either intentions or announcements of intention are under the "control" of anything.

CONCLUSION

Behaviorism is right in insisting that there must be some sort of conceptual tie between the language of mental phenomena and public circumstances and behavior. If there were not, psychological terms could not be taught, because there would be no basis for judging that our pupils employed them correctly or incorrectly. If a small child says "I am hungry" while rejecting food, we consider that he has not learned what to say. If he says it while rejecting food and going for drink, we judge that he has confused the words "thirsty" and "hungry." When on several occasions there is the right sort of correlation of behavior and circumstances with the child's utterance of a psychological term, we conclude that he is on the way towards mastering its employment. By virtue of having behavioral criteria for the truth of some third-person psychological statements (e.g., "He is hungry") in certain circumstances, we are able to determine in a good many situations whether there is a correct understanding of various psychological terms. In this way these terms are anchored in preverbal behavior; and unless it were so there would be no shared psychological language.

There is a development, however, in the employment of psychological terms which can seem astonishing, and certainly is of great conceptual importance. I refer to the fact that the employment of psychological terms outstrips their foundation in preverbal behavior. Someone who has satisfied us that he understands certain psychological terms begins to use them in first-person statements *in the absence* of the primitive, preverbal behavior that had previously served as the basis for judging that he understood those terms. He tells us that he feels ill, or angry at someone, or worried about something, when we should not have supposed so merely from his demeanor. The interesting point is that in a great many cases we will *accept* his testimony. We conclude that he is angry when, if we had been judging solely on the basis of nonverbal behavior and visible circumstances, we should not have thought it. We begin to use his testimony as a new criterion of what he is feeling and thinking, over and above and even in conflict with the earlier nonverbal criteria.

Philosophers sometimes read Wittgenstein's insistence on there being a conceptual link between statements of sensation and the primitive, natural, expressions of sensation in human behavior,[48] as implying that there is a natural, nonverbal, behavioral counterpart of *every* statement of sensation. Wittgenstein did not mean this, and it is obviously not true. A good way to see this is to imagine trying to act out, without words, "a slight soreness in my shoulder, but not enough to bother me," or "I feel more relaxed than I did this morning." This truth about sensations is even more obviously true about moods, thoughts, beliefs, intentions, emotions. Wittgenstein remarks: "We say a dog is afraid his master will beat him; but not, he is afraid his master will beat him tomorrow. Why not?"[49] A dog's cowering can be an expression of the fear of being beaten; but a dog cannot give expression to the fear that he will be beaten *tomorrow*. This latter expression of fear is reserved for creatures that have some mastery of language.

The first-person psychological sentences must be correlated with behavior up to a point. But they quickly go beyond that point. People tell us things about themselves which take us by surprise,

48. Wittgenstein, *Investigations*, e.g., paras. 244, 281, 283, 288.
49. Ibid., para. 650.

things which we should not have guessed from our knowledge of their circumstances and behavior. A behaviorist philosopher will say that if we had known more about their history, environment, and behavior, we should have been able to infer this same information. I do not believe there are any grounds for thinking so. The testimony that people give us about their intentions, plans, hopes, worries, thoughts, and feelings is by far the most important source of information we have about them. To a great extent we cannot check it against anything else and yet to a great extent we credit it. I believe we have no reason to think it is even a theoretical possibility that this self-testimony could be adequately supplanted by inferences from external and/or internal physical variables.

Within the whole body of language the category of first-person psychological sentences has peculiar importance. The puzzling status of human beings as subjects and persons is bound up with these first-person utterances, which possess the two striking characteristics I have pointed out: first, they are not, for the most part, made on the basis of any observation; second, in many cases they cannot be "tested" by checking them against physical events and circumstances *other than* the subject's own testimony. If we want to know what a man wants, what he is thinking about, whether he is annoyed or pleased, or what he has decided, the man himself is our best source of information. We ask *him*, and *he* tells us. His own testimony has a privileged status in respect to this sort of information about himself, and *not* "because he has had an extended contact with his own behavior for many years."

In the beginning of this paper I said that Rogers had not, in his contribution to the colloquium, expounded a telling criticism of behaviorism. He does, however, make some remarks which hint at the criticism which I believe to be cogent. For example, he says, by implication, that behaviorism "transforms everything it studies into an object." [50] I have argued that behaviorism fails to perceive self-testimony in a true light. It mistakenly assumes that when a man

50. Rogers, p. 113.

tells you what he wants, intends, or hopes, what he says is based on observation and, therefore, he is speaking about himself as if he were an *object of his own observation*. Behaviorism also assumes that these first-person utterances, since they are supposedly observational in nature, could theoretically be replaced by the observations of another person, although this might require "technological advances." In short, behaviorism fails to perceive that self-testimony is not replaceable, even in principle, by observations of functional relations between physical variables.[51]

51. In his brilliant review (*Language*, 35 [1959], 26–58, reprinted in *The Structure of Language*, ed. J. Fodor and J. J. Katz [Englewood Cliffs, N.J., 1964]) of Skinner's *Verbal Behavior*, Noam Chomsky shows conclusively, in my opinion, that Skinner fails to make a case for his belief that "functional analysis" is able to deal adequately with verbal behavior.

5 | The Privacy of Experience

In writings on the topic of "the privacy of experience" two themes can often be discerned, one of which I shall call "the privacy of observability," the other "the privacy of ownership." The first means that I can *observe* (or perceive, or be aware of, or know) something that no one else *can* observe (or perceive, or be aware of, or know). The second theme means that I *have* something that no one else *can* have.

The first theme is illustrated by Bertrand Russell's book *The Analysis of Mind*. Russell asks, "Can we observe anything about ourselves which we cannot observe about other people, or is everything we can observe public, in the sense that another could also observe it if suitably placed?" [1] He gives the answer that at least bodily sensations and mental images are "private": that is, "each is only observable by one observer." [2] Russell is saying that only *I* can observe or perceive *my* sensations and images: the emphasis is on the idea that there are objects that only one person can *observe*.

In other writers the emphasis is on the privacy of *ownership*. For example, Professor A. J. Ayer, in his *Language, Truth and Logic*, [3] has the theory that a *self* is nothing but a series of sense-experiences: and he says that "it is logically impossible for a sense-ex-

1. Russell, *The Analysis of Mind* (New York, 1921), p. 117.
2. Ibid., p. 118.
3. Ayer, *Language, Truth and Logic* (London, 2d ed., 1946).

perience to belong to the sense-history of more than a single self," [4]
or, as he also puts it, "all sense-experiences, and the sense-contents
which form part of them, are private to a single self." [5] In his book
The Foundations of Empirical Knowledge he retains the theory that a
self is a series of experiences, and he repeats that "it is impossible
that the same experience should be part of the history of two separate selves." [6]

Ayer was stating, in those books, the theme of the privacy of
ownership. His idea may have been (this is only a conjecture) that
since, on his theory, my experiences *make up* what I am, therefore
you and I cannot *have* the same experiences, because then there
would be only *one* of us, not two.

Some writers would not see any difference between the privacy
of observability and the privacy of ownership. For example, Ayer
in a later book, *Philosophical Essays*,[7] says: "The warrant for saying
that I can have direct knowledge of my own experiences but not
anybody's else's is just that my experiences are exclusively my
own. The reason why I cannot directly know the experiences of
another person is simply that I cannot have them." It is not clear
whether Ayer is thinking here that there is a difference between
the privacy of what I directly know (i.e., the privacy of observability) and the privacy of what I have (i.e., the privacy of ownership), or whether his view is that there is only one fact that is being
expressed in two different ways. Many philosophers would incline
toward this latter view. For they would say that what only I can be
aware of only I can have, and what only I can have only I can be
aware of: to speak of the privacy of what is observed and of the
privacy of what is owned is to speak of the same thing. It is likely
that the following remarks by Professor W. T. Stace reflect this
view:

I cannot experience anything except *my own* experience. I can see my red,
but I can never see yours. I can feel a pain in my leg. But I can never feel

4. Ibid., p. 125.　　5. Ibid., p. 128.
6. Ayer, *The Foundations of Empirical Knowledge* (New York, 1940), p. 139.
7. Ayer, *Philosophical Essays* (New York, 1954), p. 194.

the pain in your leg. I can feel my emotions, but not yours. Even if your anger infects me, so that I feel it in sympathy with you, it is yet, in so far as I feel it, *my* anger, not yours. I can never be you, nor you me. I cannot see through your eyes, nor you through mine. Even if you can telepathically transfer a mental state, say an image, from your mind to mine, yet, when I become aware of it, it is then *my* image and not yours. Even if, as some think, I can directly perceive your mind, without having to infer it from your body, still this perception of your mind will then be to me *my* perception, *my* experience.[8]

Stace seems to be saying that there is a class of things that only I can *perceive* (or experience, or be aware of), and a class of things that only I can *have*, and that these two classes coincide.

But some writers would think that there is an importance difference between the privacy of observability and the privacy of ownership. For example, consider the view stated in a recent paper by Don Locke.[9] He makes a distinction between what he calls "logical privacy" and what he calls "mental privacy." Something is "logically private" if it cannot be "owned by or shared with others."[10] This is what I called "privacy of ownership." Something is "mentally private," according to Locke, "if only one person can perceive it."[11] This is my "privacy of observability." It should be noted that Locke regards feeling a pain as *perception:* "I use 'perceive' in the wide but not extravagant sense in which feeling a pain is a species of perceiving."[12]

Locke holds that these two forms of privacy are *not* equivalent. In respect of the example of pain, he thinks that the privacy of *ownership* is a necessary truth: it is logically impossible for anyone else to *have* this pain I have. But the privacy of *observability*, he thinks, is merely a contingent truth. At the present time it is impossible for you to feel a pain of mine; but someday technological advance may make it possible for one person to feel another's pain.

Let us ask what the difference would be between my feeling *my* pain and my feeling *your* pain? Locke ought to believe that there is

8. Stace, *The Theory of Knowledge and Existence* (Oxford, 1932), p. 67.
9. D. Locke, "The Privacy of Pain," *Analysis,* 24 (1964).
10. Ibid., p. 148.   11. Ibid.   12. Ibid.

some criterion for distinguishing, from among the pains I might feel, those that would be *mine* from those that would be *yours*. And indeed Locke does believe there is such a criterion, and that it is *location*. "Identity of location," he says, is a necessary condition for the identity of bodily sensations; [13] by "identity of location" he means identity of location in physical space. Since the headache that one man feels is in a different location in physical space, namely, in a different head, than is the headache another feels, therefore they are different headaches. The criterion of *mine* and *yours* with regard to headaches, according to Locke, is that the headache *in my head* is mine, and the headache *in your head* is yours. At the present time it is not possible for me to feel your headache or toothache. But some future scientific development might make it possible, says Locke, for our respective nervous systems to be so connected that I should be able to feel the toothache in your tooth, i.e., I should be able to feel *your* toothache. We could "plug into" another's nervous system "in order to feel his pain." [14]

I want to ask whether there is any difference between *owning* bodily sensations and *observing* or *perceiving* them. As I understand it, "owning sensations" is to mean having sensations. But how are "perceiving" and "observing" to be understood? It is suspiciously unnatural to speak of "perceiving" a sensation. Let us assume that "perceiving" a sensation will mean just the same as *feeling* it. What about "observing" a sensation? This expression, too, has an odd ring. But we do speak of being aware of, or conscious of, or noticing, or paying attention to, a sensation. Let us assume that "observing" a sensation will mean some or all of these things. I will ask two questions: first, whether there is any difference between having and feeling a bodily sensation; second, whether there is any difference between having a sensation and being aware of it, or being conscious of it, or noticing it, or paying attention to it.

Considering the first question, it seems clear that there is no distinction, except verbal, between *having* and *feeling* bodily sensa-

13. Ibid., p. 149.   14. Ibid.

tions. The questions "Does he still have those twinges?" and "Does he still feel those twinges?" are used interchangeably. The doctor asks, "Are you in pain?", "Do you have pain?", "Do you feel pain?". It doesn't matter to us which set of words is used. The verification that someone has pain is identical with the verification that he feels pain. To verify that he has pain we must observe some response or reaction of his, some movement or utterance, that shows he is in pain. This same movement or utterance will also show that he *feels* pain. We cannot find out that he has pain without finding out that he feels it; and we cannot find out that he feels it without finding out that he has it. This identity of verification is one aspect of the complete identity in use of such expressions as "having a burning sensation" and "feeling a burning sensation." In applying those expressions to myself and to others, I do not know how to make a difference in my use of them.

Turning to the second question, it should be observed that a person can pay *more or less* attention to a sensation he has: he can be more or less conscious of it or aware of it. If someone is strenuously complaining of a toothache, he is sometimes admonished or advised in the following ways: "Don't think so much about it!"; "Try to take you mind off it"; "Don't pay so much attention to it." Sometimes the advice is effective: he really does succeed to some extent in taking his mind off the pain. Does it follow that he feels *less* pain? This is an interesting and difficult question which I will not pursue.

But even if it is true that the less attention a man pays to pain the less he feels, it does not follow that if he is not conscious of any pain then he feels no pain. We can think of cases in which we should be inclined to say that a man felt a sensation without being conscious of it. For example, a soundly sleeping man is jabbed in the leg with a sharp object: the leg is drawn back violently and he gasps: but his state of heavy sleep is resumed, and when he is awakened a minute or two later he has no recollection of pain. This case makes us feel pushed toward saying both that the jab *pained* him, and also that he was not *conscious* of pain. The violent movement and the gasp, together with the fact that here was a normal cause of pain, provide a criterion for saying that the jab *pained* him, i.e., he *felt* pain. His continuing state of sleep, and his negative testimony on awaking, provide a criterion for saying that he was not *conscious* of pain. There is a genuine difference in the nature of the two criteria, and therefore a reasonable basis for making this distinction. It can be employed not only in regard to animals (especially lower animals) but also in regard to human beings when they are in unconscious or semiconscious states, or are heavily distracted.

What bearing does this discussion have on the supposed distinction between the privacy of ownership and the privacy of observability? I think it is relevant only in the sense of showing what philosophers have *not* meant by this distinction. When Russell, in *The Analysis of Mind*, speaks of "observing" one's own bodily sensations, he only means *feeling* them.[15] He is not concerned, for example, with the phenomenon of paying more or less attention to a sensation, nor with the difference between feeling a sensation and being conscious of it. When Locke, too, speaks of "perceiving" pain he simply means, as already noted, feeling pain. But we have seen that there is no difference between having and feeling a bodily sensation. If the philosophical distinction between the "ownership" and the "perception" of sensation is meant to be a distinction between *having* and *feeling* sensations, then it is a distinction without a difference. Thus the themes of the privacy of ownership and the privacy of observability seem to be identical. For the remainder of this paper I will assume that these two verbally different themes of privacy do come to the same thing.

II

I return now to Locke's conception of the supposed distinction between the ownership and the perception of pain. On his own view this would be a distinction between having and feeling pain; but since there is no real distinction here, he is wrong from the

15. Russell, e.g., *Analysis of Mind*, p. 118.

start. A more interesting problem is provoked by his claim that the criterion of the ownership of pain (i.e., the criterion of *who* has pain) is the *location* of pain. I will contend that the ownership of pain is determined not by location, but by *who expresses pain*. Wittgenstein remarks: "Pain-behavior can point to a painful place—but the suffering person is the one who expresses pain." [16] The one who expresses pain, either by natural pain-behavior or by words, is the one who is in pain. If you were informed that there is a person nearby who is in pain, but you did not know which person, you would find out by finding out which one expresses pain in movements, actions, or speech.

The view that which person has pain is to be settled by finding where the pain is located puts the cart before the horse. Our discovery of where pain (other than our own) is located presupposes that we know who the subject of pain is. Knowing that *this* person is in pain, we can be guided by his pain-behavior (his flinching, limping, caressing, pointing, exclaiming) to the location of the painful area. His expressive behavior *defines*, for others, the location of the pain. The knowledge of who is in pain is logically prior to the knowledge of the location of pain. It cannot be true, as Locke thinks, that the ownership of pain is determined by the location of pain. This would make a mystery of how the location of pain is itself determined.

The fact that the ownership of pain is not fixed by its location is also proved by the empirical fact that sometimes people locate pains outside their bodies. The most familiar phenomenon under this heading, known for centuries, is the so-called "phantom limb." A person who has had a limb amputated may, for some months after, feel pains in the place where the limb used to be. He points to a place not occupied by a part of his body and declares that he feels the pain *there*. We cannot get around this phenomenon by holding that the man is not really in pain but only (mistakenly) believes he is, or by holding that the pain is not where he (mis-

16. Wittgenstein, *Philosophical Investigations*, para. 302.

takenly) believes it is but in some other place. I think we have to accept at face value his indication of the painful place. His pain really
is located in a place that is not occupied by flesh, bone, or nerves.

One may feel doubtful about this view for the following reason.
The locating of pain in empty space has the disadvantage that
much of the behavior that can be directed toward a painful place
will necessarily be missing. The man who feels pain in a phantom
limb cannot caress, protect, or favor the painful place; the pain cannot be intensified by probing that place; and so on. A substantial
amount of the behavior commonly serving to identify the location
of pain will be impossible. This may seem to prevent it from being
completely correct to say that the pain is where the man points, even
though he is not making any sort of *mistake*.

Against this objection it needs to be pointed out that there is *no
conflict of criteria* in this case. The facts are *not* these: that although
the man sincerely declares he feels pain in his leg, he does not
limp, does not flinch when the leg is probed, and so on. Such facts
might give the result that there was *no right thing to say*. There
would be a conflict between his words, and the rest of his nonverbal behavior. In the actual phantom-limb case, his declaration in
words and his nonverbal behavior of pointing are in agreement: and
there is no nonverbal behavior in disagreement. The facts are not
that he has the leg but does not limp with it, flinch when it is
probed, etc. Adequate criteria for the location of pain (both his
statement and his pointing) are satisfied. No countervailing criterion is satisfied. I do not see any sound basis for the inclination to
feel that it is not entirely correct to say that the pain is where the
man indicates.[17] This inclination may arise partly from the assumption that the location of a pain is the location of a *cause* of the
pain (and empty space can contain no cause of pain). I will proceed
to this point immediately.

It is interesting that there is a strong inclination to take the
phantom-limb case as proving that a person's pointing, limping,

17. For thoughts on this problem I am indebted both to Professor David Sachs
and to Professor Ann Wilbur Mackenzie.

favoring, protecting, and other pain-behavior, does *not* define for us the location of his pain. For example, Professor Kurt Baier says the following:

> The facts of the phantom limb clearly demonstrate that by "the place of a pain" we cannot mean the place to which we have a disposition to point. When he learns of his misfortune, the legless soldier withdraws his claim that he has a pain in his foot, although he was and still is inclined to point to the same spot, namely, the spot where the foot would be if he still had one. It is clear why the soldier withdraws this claim. It is, because, as a matter of empirical fact, the history, the fate, the life of the pain no longer depend on what happens to his foot. The doctor can move about, cut, squeeze, burn the amputated foot without thereby in any way affecting the person's pain. The pain is therefore no more "in" his foot than it is in the blanket occupying the spot where it would be if it were still his, or anywhere else. To claim that the pain is *in* the foot is therefore to imply that, causally speaking, "the key to the pain" lies in the foot. Therefore, the pain cannot be *in* the place to which the legless soldier is disposed to point. For whatever is in that place, whether his amputated foot, the bed in which he lies, or the blankets covering his body, is not "the key to the pain," not the object whose fate determines the fate of the pain. Hence we do not say that the pain is *in it*. The place to which we are disposed to point, when we have a pain, is merely the place where we believe, *rightly or wrongly*, that the pain is. The disposition to manifest "directed pain behavior" is tied to our *belief* about where the pain is, not to where the pain is. Since this belief may be erroneous, as the facts of the phantom limb show, we cannot identify the place of a pain with the place to which we are disposed to point when we have a pain.[18]

It is true that the amputated soldier may feel it a bit awkward to say that the pain is in his left foot when he knows that he has no left foot. But this is trivial. The important fact is that he will still say that the pain is *here* (pointing at a place not presently occupied by a part of his body); and Baier admits this. Baier goes wrong, I believe, in supposing that the reason the soldier will be reluctant to say that the pain is in his foot is that he no longer believes that "the fate of the pain," as Baier puts it, depends on what happens to his

18. Kurt Baier, "The Place of A Pain," *Philosophical Quarterly*, 14 (1964), p. 140.

foot (or what used to be his foot). Baier thinks that the notion of the location of a pain involves the notion of the location of the *cause* of the pain. He says, "To claim that the pain is *in* the foot is therefore to imply that, *causally speaking*, 'the key to the pain' lies in the foot." [19]

It is true that in a huge number of cases the bodily cause of a pain has the same location as the pain. But there are familiar cases in which this is not so. The "key" to a headache is sometimes a nerve in the neck; and the so-called "referred" pains of angina are located in the shoulder rather than in the heart where the bodily damage is. Even if we ignore these empirical facts, we can see that it is wrong to think that locating pain is the same as locating the (or a) bodily cause of pain. These are different concepts. A man may give us the location of his pain without having any beliefs at all about the location of its bodily cause. He need not even assume that it has a bodily cause. (He might think it was "psychosomatic.") The notion of the location of the bodily cause of pain is a good deal more sophisticated that is the notion of the location of pain. The first notion relies on past experience and experiment; the second does not. [20]

19. Ibid., my italics. There is a similarity, and also a dissimilarity, between Baier's view and the view of Thomas Reid. According to Reid, pain, being a *sensation*, can exist only "in the mind," not in the body. When the ordinary man says he has pain in his toe, he is making a complex assertion, one part of which is that he feels pain, and the other part is that the *cause* of the pain is in the toe. "When we consider the sensation of pain by itself, without any respect to its cause, we cannot say with propriety, that the toe is either the place or the subject of it. But it ought to be remembered that, when we speak of pain in the toe, the sensation is combined in our thought, with the cause of it, which really is in the toe" (Thomas Reid, *Works*, ed. W. Hamilton [Edinburgh, 1858], *Essays on the Intellectual Powers*, Essay II, chap. 18, pp. 319–320). Baier does not hold that we cannot say, "with propriety," that our sensations are located in our bodies. But he does hold, with Reid, that when I say I have pain in my toe, part of what I assert is that the (or a) *cause* of the pain is in my toe. If this part of my assertion turned out to be mistaken, then I would have a mistaken belief that I have pain in my toe.

20. One could be misled by the fact that sometimes we probe a painful area in order to discover the point of maximum tenderness, i.e., the "center" of the painful area. Sometimes we call this center of pain the "source" of the pain. Since the word "source" commonly has a causal meaning, this way of speaking might give a philoso-

III

To summarize our progress thus far: (1) Feeling a sensation and having it are the same. (2) Which person has pain (the problem of ownership) is not defined by the location of pain, but instead the location of pain is defined by the directed pain-behavior (verbal and nonverbal) of the person who is in pain. (3) The concepts of cause of, and location of, pain must not be confused.

I turn now to the question of the "privacy" of pain. This is the idea that it is impossible that two people should have (or feel) the *same* pain. I believe this idea is pure illusion. In the *Investigations* there occurs this remark: "In so far as it makes *sense* to say that my pain is the same as his, it is also possible for us both to have the same pain." [21] Wittgenstein is implying that there is *not* some sense of the expressions "same pain," such that you and I *cannot* have the same pain. This goes counter to what many philosophers think. They think that there is *a* sense in which you and I cannot have the same pain. They will say that there is an ambiguity in the expression "same pain." On the one hand, this may mean "qualitative similarity" or "exact similarity"; on the other hand, it may mean "numerical identity." It is in this latter sense of "same pain," they say, that it is impossible for you and me to have the same pain.

Ayer takes this view in his *Philosophical Essays*. [22] He allows that two people may "share" the same fear. But, he adds, "To say that the feeling is shared is to say that the two feelings are qualitatively similar and that they have the same ostensible object: it is not to say that they are numerically identical." He admits there is some difficulty about how we are to *count* the feelings. But he declares that it is simply a convention "that we are to say that there are two feelings and not one, just because there are two persons." [23]

In *The Problem of Knowledge*, Ayer says, "It is true that one does

pher the idea that what the probing determines is the bodily cause (i.e., the "source") of that pain. In reality what has been determined is merely "where it hurts the most."

21. Wittgenstein, *Investigations*, para. 253.
22. Ayer, *Philosophical Essays*, p. 194.   23. Ibid., p. 195.

quite frequently speak of different persons sharing the same thoughts or feelings, but it would generally be held that what is meant by this is that these thoughts or feelings are similar, or proceed from similar causes, not that they are literally the same." [24] And in his book *The Concept of a Person*, he says, "Headaches are private: it does not make sense to say that several people are feeling the same headache." [25]

Peter Strawson, in his *Individuals*, holds that with regard to "states of consciousness" there is a "logically nontransferable kind of ownership." He says that if we consider "the requirements of identifying reference in speech to *particular* states of consciousness, or private experiences, we see that such particulars cannot be thus identifyingly referred to except as the states or experiences *of* some identified *person*. States, or experiences, one might say, *owe* their identity as particulars to the identity of the person whose states or experiences they are." And he declares that it follows from this "that it is logically impossible that a particular state or experience in fact possessed by someone should have been possessed by someone else." [26]

Let us consider the distinction between "exact similarity" and "numerical identity" to which these philosophers allude. We can certainly think of cases in which we want to make use of this distinction, or something like it. With cigars, for example. If it were said that after dinner Petersen and Hansen smoked the same cigar, the remark could be ambiguous. It could mean that the cigar Hansen smoked was not distinguishable in respect to size, shape, color, or brand from the cigar Petersen smoked. We could express this, in ordinary speech, by saying that they smoked "the identical cigar." We say, for example, that "Six ladies at the ball were wearing the identical dress." What these remarks tend to mean is that *two* cigars were being smoked by Petersen and Hansen, and that neither cigar had any feature that distinguished it from the other;

24. Ayer, *The Problem of Knowledge* (New Yrok, 1956), p. 226.
25. Ayer, *The Concept of a Person* (New York, 1963), p. 50.
26. Strawson, *Individuals* (London, 1959), p. 97.

and among the dresses at the ball there were *six* that were indistinguishable—"You could not tell them apart."

But one could mean something different by saying that the two men smoked the same ("the identical") cigar: namely, that altogether only one cigar was being smoked by them: (they passed it back and forth like a peace pipe). The expression "numerical identity" is supposed to take care of this case. We are to say that the two men smoked "numerically the same" cigar. I suspect that this phrase is not actually used in ordinary speech but has been invented by philosophers. Still, this does not prevent it from being a useful phrase. If you have told me that A and B are smoking the same cigar at the dinner table, and I ask "Numerically the same?", you could understand me to be asking how many cigars, altogether, are being smoked by A and B.

The fact that there is a distinction between exact similarity and numerical identity that can be made in regard to cigars and dresses does not imply that it can be made in regard to anything whatever. You can say that two people have the same ("the identical") *style* in playing tennis; but what if I asked whether you meant that A's style is exactly like B's style or that A and B have numerically the same style? You would not understand this question. You informed me that A and B have exactly the same style of play: there cannot be a *further* question as to whether A's style is numerically identical with B's style. With the cigars and dresses there can be this further question: A and B appeared in the same dress at different times during the evening, but was it numerically the same dress?

Thus a question of the form "*x* and *y* are exactly alike, but is *x* numerically the same as *y*?" makes sense with some values for *x* and *y*, but not for others. If we substitute "A's cigar" for "*x*" and "B's cigar" for "*y*," we obtain a sensible question. We understand that it might turn out that A and B had altogether only one cigar, or that they had two. In regard to some other sorts of things, e.g., tennis style, this further question is meaningless.

Let us consider whether this further question has any meaning with respect to colors. Surface A and surface B have exactly the same color, i.e., they are "identical" or "indistinguishable" in color. Can there be a further question as to whether the color of A is numerically identical with the color of B? What would it mean? Given that the color of one area is indistinguishable from the color of another area, what more can be asked? Despite what we are tempted to think, there is not a sense of "same color" such that the color of one place *cannot* be the same as the color of another place. It is one of the most truistic of truisms that the very same shade of color can be many places at the same time. In such cases there are numerically different colored areas colored the same shade.

Let us turn to the psychological realm, considering first *opinions*. Two people can be of the same opinion, e.g., that a summer in the mountains would be more enjoyable than a summer at the seashore. But once you know that A and B have the same opinion, would you know what it meant to further find out whether A's opinion was numerically the same as or different from B's? You would not. In this respect opinions are different from cigars and dresses, and are more like styles and colors.

What about sudden thoughts? Surely a sudden thought is a "mental event," if anything is. Two people might have the same sudden thought at the same time, e.g., the thought that the stove has not been turned off. Is there now a further question as to whether altogether they have *two* thoughts, exactly alike, or just *one* thought? What would be the difference?

My suddenly thinking that the stove has not been turned off is a different occurrence, or event, from *your* suddenly thinking the same thing. But it does not follow that I *have* something which you do not have. It cannot be said, for example, that I had my having the thought that p, whereas you did not. To say "I had my having the thought that p" is to speak gibberish. It is no better to say "I had my thinking the thought that p, but you did not have it." What can be said is "I had the sudden thought that p": but then you could have had the same.

Let us turn to *bodily sensations*. Here the temptation is great (in-

deed, overwhelming) to suppose that there is a sense of "same sensation" in which two people *cannot* have the same. But the case is
really no different from that of styles, colors, opinions, and sudden
thoughts. If the description of my backache is the same as the
description of yours, then you and I have the same backache. This
is how the expression "same backache" is used. If your backache
answers to a different description then it is different. There is no
other sense of "same" and "different" in regard to sensations. There
is no sense of "different sensation" such that my sensation and your
sensation *must* be different, just as there is no sense of "different
color" such that the color of two areas *must* be different.

It is worth noting that descriptions of sensations can be imper-
sonal. A sensation might be described as "a throbbing pain in the
shoulder." Personal pronouns do not have to enter into verbal descriptions of sensations. The descriptions of sensations in a medical
book would not say *whose* sensations they were, yet they could be
complete descriptions.

By "a description of a sensation" I mean what is ordinarily
meant. In describing a bodily sensation one would mention
whether it was dull or sharp or throbbing, whether the intensity of
it waxed and waned, what its location was, and so on. Many things
that were *true of* a sensation (e.g., that I had it on February 22nd,
in the afternoon) would *not* belong to a *description* of it.

There is an inclination to think that A's sensation and B's sensation must have different descriptions: for A says, "The ache is in
my shoulder," and although B utters the same words, he refers to a
shoulder that is numerically different from the shoulder referred to
by A. Thus A and B give *different locations* to their sensations; and
so they describe them differently.

This is wrong. Giving the location of one's sensation is not locating it in the space of physics or astronomy, but in a space of sensations that has one's own body as its frame of reference. If A locates
a sensation in his space of sensation (e.g., in his right shoulder),
and B locates a sensation in the corresponding place in B's space of

sensation (e.g., in *his* right shoulder), then B's sensation is in the *same* place as A's sensation. If B located his sensation in a *non*corresponding place (e.g., his right foot), then B's sensation would be in a *different* place from A's. *This is how we use* the expressions "same place," "different place," in regard to sensations. Therefore, A and B are *not* giving different descriptions when each says, "in my shoulder."

Descriptions of sensations provide the criteria of identity for sensations.[27] Since your sensation can have the same description as mine, you and I can have the same sensation. Contrary to Strawson's view, the identity of sensations does not depend on the identity of the persons who have them.[28] It is not a characterizing feature of a sensation that *I* have it. As Wittgenstein remarks, "In pain I distinguish intensity, location, etc., but no owner." [29]

If being *mine* were a characterizing feature of a sensation I have, then I ought to be able to say, "I have a pain that is mine," just as I can say, "I have a pain that is throbbing." But actually the first remark means no more than that I have a pain—which has yet to be described.[30] The first remark ought to be a contribution to the description of the sensation; but it is not.

Thus we make a senseless move when we assert, "Another person cannot have *my* sensation." If we were to provide a description of the sensation (e.g., "a throbbing pain in the shoulder") it would be plainly false that another person cannot have *that*. If no description is provided, or in the offing, then we have not said anything.

So it is a mistake to think that if you and I have the same sensation this can only mean that your sensation is exactly like mine, not that it is *numerically* the same. In so far as we understand the con-

---

27. It might be objected that there are indescribable sensations. And indeed we do want to say, sometimes, that a sensation is "indescribable." But still a lot can be said about the sensation: for one thing, what it is *not;* and also that it is "indescribable."

28. Strawson, p. 97.

29. Wittgenstein, *Philosophische Bemerkungen* (Frankfurt am Main, 1964), p. 94.

30. Cf. ibid., p. 91.

cept "exactly alike but numerically different," it has no application to sensations.[31] Nor to any other "contents of consciousness," such as images, feelings, or emotions. Given that the description of your image, feeling, or emotion is the same as mine, there cannot be a *further* question as to whether yours is *different* from mine. One could express the point by saying that contents of consciousness have only *generic* identity and not *numerical* identity.

I hope it will not be thought insulting if I say that all of us are influenced by very *crude* imagery. We tend to think of a *mind* as an intangible volume of space, and of the *contents* of that mind as located inside that volume of space. Another mind is a different volume of space, and its contents are numerically different from the contents of any other mind because they are located in a different space. I believe our strong temptation to assume that one person's thoughts, feelings, and "experiences" cannot be "numerically" the same as another's springs in part from this imagery—although that is not the whole story.

The assumption that your sensation and mine must be numerically different is a *bad* mistake, philosophically speaking, because it

---

31. I am not holding that there are no cases at all in which the question "Numerically the same?" will have application to sensations. Suppose, for example, that a doctor tells me that each time Petersen and his wife come to see him, "they complain of the same sensation." I might ask, "Numerically the same?" What I might want to know is whether there is a sensation that only *one* of them has and of which both of them complain; or whether there is a sensation *both* of them have and of which both of them complain. My question is a request for information as to whether one or both of them have the sensation to which the doctor refers; and this is an intelligible question. (I owe this example to Professor John Cook.) One can easily think of still other cases in which those words would express an intelligible question. The philosophically interesting case, as far as the problem of privacy is concerned, is the one where I *know* (i.e., it is given) that A has a sensation of a certain description and B has one of the same description. It is in *this* case that my question "Do they have numerically the same or numerically different sensations?" is unintelligible—despite our metaphysical conviction that it *must* be intelligible and indeed that we know the answer. To think that because there are two people there must be two sensations is exactly like thinking that because there are two areas colored a certain shade there must be two colors.

embodies the idea that the contents of your mind (your thoughts, feelings, sensations) are hidden from me. Thus it puts us on the road to skepticism about other minds, and even to solipsism.

Of course it is often impossible for me to find out another's thoughts or feelings. This might be because the other person does not trust me or is afraid of me, or because he has greater intelligence, sensitivity, or depth than I have. It is not because the contents of his mind are "numerically different" from mine.

If the distinction between "the same" and "numerically the same" *were* to be given an application to sensations, then we should have to *make up* criteria for it. Our ordinary speech contains none. It is interesting that we are drawn in different directions when it comes to stipulating criteria for the numerical identity of sensations. This comes out plainly enough in the imaginary case of the Siamese twins who share a common limb, e.g., a hand. Suppose that each of them complained of a pain in exactly the same spot in their common hand, each giving the same description of the pain he felt. Would there be one or two pains in that hand? Now there is some inclination to count the number of pains by counting the number of spatial locations of pain. By this rule there would be *one* pain felt by two people. On the other hand, there is some inclination to count the number of pains by counting the number of persons in pain. By this rule there would be *two* pains in the same spot in that hand. Which rule is the right one? Neither. Our ordinary concept of pain does not embody either rule. And if it came to adopting one of these rules, in order to solve the problem of the Siamese twins, it would be as arbitrary to choose the one as the other.

Despite the mountain of confusion on the subject, I hope my discussion has shown that our ordinary concept of pain embodies the following features: (1) having and feeling pain are the same; (2) the criterion of which person has pain is which person expresses pain, and not where the pain is located; (3) there is no sense of the expression "same pain" such that it is impossible for two people to have the same pain.[32]

IV

I wish to raise the question of what it is that gives rise to the illusion of the privacy of pain, i.e., to the mistaken inclination to assume that you and I cannot have the same. The persistent strength of this illusion is something that needs to be explained. I believe it is provoked by certain features of our use of the word "pain." In Wittgenstein's metaphors, they are features of the "grammar" of the word, or of the "language-game," with the word. I think the facts that give rise to the illusion of privacy would be the following: (a) You can be *in doubt* as to whether I am in pain, but I cannot; (b) You can *find out* whether I am in pain, but I can-

---

32. This remark may not be *literally* true. We do speak of "instances" or "cases" of headache. The criteria of identity for instances or cases of headache, would include the identity of the owners. If two people each had headache of description ∅, then there would be two *cases* of headache ∅, i.e., numerically different cases of the same headache. Your case of headache would, necessarily, be numerically different from my case of headache.

It is possible that economy of language sometimes leads us to use the expression "different headache" when what we mean is *different case of the same headache*, and also to say "same headache" when what we mean is *same case of the same headache*. Whether or not we actually do this, we *could* do it. I shall call this a "secondary" sense of the expressions "different headache" and "same headache." Within the phrase "different case of the same headache," the expression "same headache" occurs in its primary sense. In this primary sense, the criteria of identity for headaches include location, intensity, etc., but not the identity of the owners. In the secondary sense, the criteria of identity do include the identity of the owners.

I am confident that when Ayer says "Headaches are private: several people cannot feel the same headache" (*The Concept of A Person*, p. 50), he *wants* to be speaking of "same headache" in the primary sense. If we construed his remark as being about the secondary sense of "same headache," we should be entitled to translate it as follows: "Several people cannot feel the same case of headache." But then we should want to object to speaking of "feeling a *case* of headache." What does it mean? It isn't even English. The same holds for "feel an instance of headache." Thus if we are going to understand Ayer's remark, we should interpret it as using "same headache" in the *primary* sense of the expression. But then the remark that "several people cannot feel the same headache," although good English, is not true. In the primary sense of "same headache" several people can feel the same headache.

not; and (c) You can be *mistaken* as to whether I am in pain, but I cannot.

The most surprising thing about this set of facts is what *I* cannot do. *I* cannot be in doubt, or find out, or be mistaken as to whether *I* am in pain. Of course, someone could fail to understand the English word "pain," but that is of no interest. Wittgenstein remarks that if someone said, "Oh, I know what the word 'pain' means; what I don't know is whether *this*, that I have now, is pain," we should be at a loss to understand him.[33] This remark of Wittgenstein's is a little misleading, since it can actually be informative for a person to say, "I don't know whether this is pain." It shows us that his sensation is *hard to classify*. He might be telling us that his sensation lies in the borderland between a pain and a tickle, say, or a pain and an ache. His remarks would be a partial characterization of his sensation. It would be a contribution to the description of his sensation.

To appreciate Wittgenstein's point, let us make the following two assumptions: first, that the speaker understands the use of the word "pain"; second, that he is not characterizing his sensation as borderline. Given these assumptions, "that expression of doubt does not belong to the language-game," as Wittgenstein puts it.[34]

Notice that "the expression of doubt" to which he refers is a speaker's expression of doubt about *his own case*. If a speaker is referring to someone else, there is no problem: "I don't know if he has pain" is not prima facie a logically troubling remark. Furthermore, as we saw earlier, there can even be cases in which we should be *inclined* to say something of the following sort: "The jab pained him but he was not conscious of the pain, or was not aware that he felt pain, or did not know that he felt pain." This implies that there can be cases in which we should be *inclined* to say: "He is not aware (does not know) that he has pain." I think it is not definitely settled that such a remark is excluded from language.

But what is true is that a person who understands the language

33. *Investigations*, para. 288.   34. Ibid.

cannot himself express doubt, or ignorance, as to whether he has pain. One is not permitted to say "I do not know if I have pain" (unless one is characterizing a sensation as borderline). A genuine expression of doubt is not allowed.

This is a striking and important fact; and I interpret Wittgenstein as pointing it out. If a man understands the word "influenza," and even if he has influenza, he is allowed to express a doubt as to whether he has influenza. But he is not allowed to express a doubt as to whether he has pain. He is not permitted to say "I don't know if I have pain," or "I believe I have pain but I may be wrong," or "I intend to find out whether I have pain." Why is this?

v

It leaves us discontented to be told that the first-person expression of doubt does not belong to the language-game with the word "pain." We should like an explanation of *why* this is so. It is my conjecture that the philosophers who espouse the thesis of the privacy of pain are wanting to *explain* why it is that the expression of doubt about one's own case is missing from the game with the word "pain." The *reason* for this, they want to say, is that when a person is in pain, he has direct and immediate *knowledge* that he is in pain. This is why he cannot be in doubt, cannot be mistaken, and cannot find out: for as soon as he is in pain he *knows* it.

This explanation is unsatisfactory. The utterance "I know I am in pain" is just as queer as the utterance "I don't know if I am in pain." To be sure, we can think of cases in which it would be quite natural to say "I know I have a toothache." This might be an emphatic way of stating that I have a toothache (a sort of rhetorical flourish). And there is the case where the dentist has injected more than a normal amount of novocaine, but you still complain of pain, and he asks, "Are you *sure* it still hurts?": to which you reply, "I *know* it still hurts." Possibly he suspected that you were pretending or exaggerating, and your reply assured him you were not. Or perhaps your reply just meant, "Don't talk nonsense!", in which case it was a logical or philosophical comment, and an appropriate one!

When the phrase "I know" is prefixed to a sentence it is normally a *useful* prefix. It does a job. One job it can do is to inform the auditor that the speaker has *grounds* for asserting that *p*, and is not making his claim from mere prejudice or unsupported rumor. Another job it can do is to inform the auditor that the speaker is an *authority* on the general subject matter of the statement *p*. ("I know his agreement to purchase is illegal." "How do you know?" "I am a lawyer.") Or this prefix can inform the auditor that the speaker is in a *privileged position* to say whether *p* is true. ("I know the lady snores." "How do you know?" "She is my wife.")

I think everyone feels that the sentence "I know I am in pain" is a rather queer thing to say; and some would hold that it is senseless. I wish to argue that it *is* senseless. But I do not mean that I perceive, as it were, a clash of meanings in my mind when I say the words. I mean that in this case the prefix "I know" cannot do any of its normal jobs. Thus there is a good and sufficient reason for excluding the combination of words "I know I am in pain" from language.[35] For the prefix does no work.

None of the previously mentioned jobs can be done by this prefix when it is attached to the sentence "I have pain." It cannot serve the purpose of informing you that I have *grounds* for saying I have pain. For what could the grounds be, other than that I *feel* pain? There is, however, no distinction of meaning between "I feel pain" and "I have pain." Thus it would be a redundancy for me to put forward the fact that I feel pain, as my grounds for saying I have pain. The only plausible "grounds," therefore, are not *grounds*.[36]

Nor can my use of the I-know prefix inform you that I am an *au-*

35. "To say, 'This combination of words makes no sense' excludes it from the sphere of language and thereby bounds the domain of language. But when one draws a boundary it may be for various kinds of reason" (ibid., para. 499).

36. Compare with this case: My grounds for saying I have a hole in my tooth are that I *feel* a hole in my tooth. There is no redundancy here.

thority on the question of whether I have pain. An authority can be *proved* to be an authority. His answers can be checked out, independently of his say-so, and it can be determined that he does not make mistakes, or hardly ever does so, in his subject (e.g., the history of the Civil War). But since we do not know what it means for a person who understands English to *believe mistakenly* that he has pain,[37] the notion of a person's proving an authority on this question is also meaningless.

For the same reason a person cannot be said to be in a *privileged position* with regard to the question of whether he is in pain. Generally speaking, a husband is in a privileged position with regard to the question of whether his wife snores. Yet we can easily understand, in various ways, how he might be wrong. This is what we do not understand in the case of one's own pain. So the notion of being in a privileged position really has no application here.

Ayer admits that prefixing "I am in pain" with "I know" makes an otherwise "respectable" sentence "appear somewhat ridiculous." [38] He goes on to say: "But the reason for this, surely, is not that the claim to knowledge is inapplicable in these cases, but rather it is superfluous. We find it silly for someone to tell us that he knows that he is in pain, because if he is in pain we take it for granted that he knows it." [39]

Well, we really do take it for granted that the people we have dealings with in daily life *know their own names.* Experience teaches us that it is the normal thing for an adult person to be able to say that his name is so-and-so and to be *right*. So I do take it for granted that the people riding with me in the bus know their names. I am justified in making this assumption. I do not make it

---

37. In the case of the sleeper who was jabbed in the leg, our inclination was to say that he was not conscious of pain he felt. It was not a case of his believing (mistakenly) that he did not feel pain.

38. Ayer, *The Concept of A Person*, p. 59.

39. Ibid. I have also heard it said that the reason we do not say, "I know I'm in pain," is that it *is so easy to tell* whether one is in pain: it is as easy as remembering one's name—perhaps even easier.

in the case of small children, and sometimes it goes wrong in the case of grown-ups. This shows that Ayer has not given a correct explanation of the "ridiculous" appearance of the sentence "I know I'm in pain." We do not "take for granted" that if a man is in pain he knows it. Experience could not justify this "assumption": for we do not know what it would mean for a person who understands the words to be *wrong* when he says "I am in pain." [40]

This utterance should not be thought of as the report of an observation of something whose ontological status is completely independent of the utterance. The utterance is itself an expression of sensation, just as flinchings, grimaces, and outcries are expressions of sensation. If the occurrence of this utterance is an expression of sensation then it serves as a criterion of sensation, just as does natural pain-behavior. [41] But then, to produce a case of a man's mistakenly believing he feels pain will not be possible. The nearest approach to this would be a *conflict* between his utterance ("I'm in pain") and his other behavior (a conflict of criteria), producing a case where it would be neither right nor wrong to say he feels pain. This would fall short of providing a case in which he was *mistaken*. Thus there cannot be a consistent criterion of the latter.

When "I know" is prefixed to "I have pain" it cannot do any of the jobs that this prefix normally does in speech. It really is a knob that does not turn anything. [42] The fundamental reason for this is that it is not a genuine possibility that a person who understands the words should be in error when he says he has pain. This prevents the prefix from fulfilling its normal purpose. I would

40. Ayer gives the following "proof" that if we are in pain we know it, namely, that one can tell lies about one's sensations. For "to tell a lie is not just to make a false statement: it is to make a statement that one knows to be false; and this implies denying what one knows to be true" (ibid., p. 60). I should take this as a proof that telling a lie is not, in all cases, stating what one knows to be false. The word "lying," like the word "game" is applied over a broad range of diverse cases.

41. Cf. my *Knowledge and Certainty* (Englewood Cliffs, N.J., 1963; republished Ithaca, N.Y., 1975), p. 140.

42. Wittgenstein, *Investigations*, paras. 270, 271.

apply here a remark from the *Tractatus:* "Signs that serve no purpose are logically meaningless." [43]

Yet, when we philosophize about sensation, we have a strong
desire to assert "If I am in pain I *must know* it." Why is this? I think
we are trying to point out the unacceptability of the supposition
that a man who either definitely does have pain, or definitely does
not have pain, and who understands the words, should truthfully
declare, "I don't know if I have pain." We are not going to accept
this as a possibility. If that is *all* we mean when we assert, "If I
have pain I *must know* it," then I do not want to make any objection
to this use of the sentence. We are expressing a logical or philosophical observation that embodies a correct appreciation of the
concept of sensation. [44]

It will be recalled that the proponent of the privacy of experience
was going to *explain* why the expression of doubt "I don't know if I
have pain" is not in the language-game. His explanation consisted
in asserting, "If I am in pain I *must know* it." But we see that the
only true thing he can mean is that the expression of doubt is ruled
out. If this is what his assertion comes to, then he is not explaining
why the expression of doubt is excluded from the language of sensation. He is merely saying over again that it it excluded.

The theme of the privacy of pain may also be thought to explain
why it is that you can be in doubt, can be mistaken, and can find
out, that I have pain, whereas *I* cannot. This would be because you
cannot have, or feel, *my* sensation. You cannot have "direct"
knowledge of my sensation, but only "indirect" knowledge by way
of my behavior and words. This attempt at explanation is as unsatisfactory as the previous one. As we saw, you can have, and feel,
the very sensation I have. (Do not protest, "But I can't feel your

43. Wittgenstein, *Tractatus Logico-Philosophicus*, trans. D. F. Pears and B. F.
McGuinness (New York, 1961), #5.47321.

44. In actual practice our meaning tends not to be so pure. Mixed in with this
true perception of the "grammar" of sensation, there will be the temptation to think
one has grounds, or is an authority, or has an unobstructed view of one's sensation,
and so on. I suspect that the phrase "privileged access" usually indicates such a mix-
ture.

feeling of it," for what could that mean?) Also we saw that in the sentence "I know I have pain" the "I know" does not serve any purpose: consequently, I cannot say that I know "directly" that I have pain; and so you cannot say, in contrast, that you know "*only* indirectly" that I have pain.

In addition, this attempt at explanation embodies a picture of my sensations as *hidden* from you. But then it undermines itself. For part of what it was going to explain is how it is that you can *find out* what my sensations are, whereas *I* cannot. But the picture it carries seems to say that you *cannot* find out my sensations.

VI

The philosophical theme of the privacy of sensation is a complete failure if conceived as an explanation of the grammar of sensation. But can there be no explanation at all? I confess that I, too, feel some discontent with the statement that this is simply how the game is played. What I conceive to be a kind of explanation, and one that satisfies me, is to see what the consequences would be for our concept of a *person*, if the grammar of sensation (or of thinking or intending) were different in the respect that the expression of doubt, which has no place in the language-game, *were* to have a place in it.

What I am trying to imagine is that I could be in doubt or mistaken as to whether *I* have pain, just as you can be; and also that I could find out whether *I* have pain, in the same way that you can. In short, I am trying to imagine that I should be in the same position as you are with regard to the question of whether *I* have pain. I want to see what the results would be if the asymmetry of our positions should be abolished. Your position is that you observe my behavior and listen to my words in order to find out if I have pain. So I will imagine that I too will observe my own behavior and listen to my own words, to find out if I have pain. If I cannot observe my behavior or hear my words, I shall be in doubt, just as you would be. In the present language-game, if another wants to know whether I have pain, he will ask me. So I will imagine that, in the projected game, I shall sometimes ask myself, "Does it hurt?" If I reply, "Yes, it does," then I shall know that I have pain, my evidence being *that I myself said so!* As things are, others sometimes question my sincerity. So I shall question my own sincerity. I shall dispute with myself, and I may or may not convince myself. Suppose I believe I am a liar: then, on the one hand, I shall say I have pain, but, on the other hand, deny it. Imagine the possibility that someone, noticing my exclamations and gestures of pain, should hurry to my aid, but I should inform him that in my opinion I do not have pain at all, or at least I am probably exaggerating; and I should urge him not to be concerned about me—yet at the same time I should continue to groan and writhe and implore him to help me!

It is clear enough that these would be bewildering phenomena. At best they would indicate a split personality—two persons, as it were, inhabiting one body.[45] At worst, they would mean complete lunacy. It is evident, furthermore, that our concepts of sensation would have no application to such a case. If I behaved in this weird way it would not be right to say I was in pain, nor right to say the opposite. Nor even right to say that I was *in doubt* as to whether I was in pain. This behavior would diverge too far from the normal. Our concepts of sensation and emotion, of belief and doubt, grow out of certain regular patterns of behavior and circumstances that are frequently repeated in human life. Our concepts are taught, and mastered, by reference to those patterns. The concepts can be extended gradually to new patterns that resemble the old. But they could not be extended to cover the phenomena we have been imagining. Those phenomena would not be coherent expressions of anything.

I have been trying to explain why we do not have the concepts of doubting, being mistaken, or finding out, whether *oneself* has pain. It is an odd sort of "explanation," and one may be reluctant to call

45. Cf. Wittgenstein's remark: "If I listened to the words of my mouth, I might say that someone else was speaking out of my mouth"; and also: "My relation to my own words is wholly different from other people's" (*Investigations*, p. 192).

it by that name. Whatever we call it, it provides a kind of clarification that is often required in philosophy, namely, to make a perplexing fact less perplexing by pointing out the part it plays in supporting a familiar structure. In the present case, the clarification comes to the following: if we try to imagine what it would be like if doubting, making a mistake, and finding out, concerning one's own sensations, were to occur (and I do not mean merely that, for example, the words "I don't know if I have pain" should be uttered, but also that there should occur both the spontaneous behavior and deliberate actions by which doubt is expressed, and the inquiries, observations, assurances, by which doubt is removed)—if we try to imagine such behavior, we see that it could not be accommodated under the headings we use in describing the attitudes and feelings of people.

We have tried to imagine what it would be like if the expression of doubt did belong to the grammar of sensation. Similar results will be obtained with the grammar of *intention*. Imagine someone learning from his own present movements and speech what his intentions are! If he put forth a statement about his present intention, based on such observations, would you have learned his intention? Does he *have* an intention?

Or imagine trying to carry on a conversation with someone who continuously infers from his own words and gestures what he *means!* Or picture someone who watches his own bodily movements to find out what he *wants!*

A person expresses feelings, beliefs, intentions, by action and by word. We look to him for information about his thoughts and intentions. He is our primary source of information about himself. (But only if his disclosures are *not* based on his observations of his own words and movements.) His behavior and utterances reveal to us his experiences, wishes, and aims (insofar as they are revealed). And accordingly, we respond with sympathy, or reproach, or indignation, or encouragement. We concert our own plans with his, or we seek to frustrate him. These are ways in which we respond to people and engage with them.

If some humanlike creature exhibited behavior of the sort we have imagined, his movements and utterances would not reveal to us any experiences, intentions, or sensations. And they would not provide a foundation for any human attitude toward him—of sympathy or annoyance, of reliance or distrust, of agreement or disagreement. To the extent that he exhibited behavior approximating the behavior of being in doubt as to whether he himself feels pain (or wants or intends something), and the connected behavior of trying to remove the doubt by observing his own movements and utterances, he could not appear to us as a person! This shows that it is essential to the concept of a person that the expression of doubt should not occur.

Thus the explanation of why the expression of doubt is excluded from language is not that each person has something, or feels or knows something, that another person cannot have, feel, or know—the explanation is not that experience is "private." The explanation is that the expression of doubt could not fit coherently into the structure of our concept of a person. The excluding of it from working language is no superficial point of grammar or semantics, but a matter of deep philosophical importance. For it is an aspect of the asymmetry between your position and mine, with respect to the question of what *I* feel or think or intend. This asymmetry is a necessary feature of the concept of a person.

6 | *Wittgenstein on the Nature of Mind*

Suppose you have two old friends, both named Tom, and you are writing to one of them. Both are ardent fishermen, and your letter tells about a recent fishing exploit of your own. Thus the content of the letter is suitable for either of them. One of them lives in Buffalo and the other in Omaha. But you have not yet addressed the envelope. Your letter begins with the greeting "Dear Tom" and ends with "Best regards. Hope to hear from you soon," followed by your signature. Let us suppose it is to the Tom in Omaha you are writing. What does your writing to *him* rather than to the other Tom consist in? What connects your letter with the one and not the other? Wittgenstein presses these question on us.[1]

Consider another example: you motioned with your hand in the direction of two people, A and B, and said "Come here." It was A you meant, not B. What went on which made it the case that you meant A?[2] Another example: you hear a piano being tuned and at the same time you have a headache. You say, "It will soon stop." What would be the difference between meaning the piano-tuning and meaning the headache?[3] Or, while walking with a companion you point toward a flower and exclaim "Look!" Let us say that you meant the flower's color, and not its shape or size or species. What did that difference consist in?[4]

1. Wittgenstein, *Zettel*, para. 7.   2. Ibid., para. 22.
3. Wittgenstein, *Philosophical Investigations*, para. 666.
4. Ibid., paras. 33–35.

In these examples a person *meant* something. Closely related is the notion of *intention*. Consider an example of the latter: in conversation you were interrupted. You were going to say, "So I must leave by ten o'clock." In what form did your intention to say those words exist before you said them? [5]

We feel that we should be able to answer these questions. Yet we are frustrated, since none of the answers that occur to us carry much conviction. We think, halfheartedly, that perhaps your writing to the one Tom rather than to the other consisted in your having an image of the one but not of the other, as you wrote the letter. But should we really want to say that you would not have been writing to the Tom of Omaha unless you had an image of him? Surely not. And in the example in which you motioned in the direction of A and B, and said "Come here," but it was A you meant, not B—should we say that this consisted in your fixing your attention on A? But your attention might not have been fixed on A. You might have been thinking about B: you were watching the expression on his face, hoping that he would not be offended by your choosing to speak to A first. In the example of the simultaneous headache and piano-tuning, would it be the case that you meant the headache when you said "It will soon stop," if your attention was concentrated on it more than on the piano-tuning? Could the question arise for you as to whether your attention was sufficiently concentrated on the headache in order for you to have meant it? [6]

We find that we are unable to specify what it was that its being a letter to the one Tom rather than to the other consisted in; or what went on when you motioned and said "Come here" which was your *meaning* that A should come and not B. We cannot say in what form your intention to say a sentence existed before you said it. We cannot seem to give an account of what you did, at the time you were pointing at the flower, such that your meaning its color consisted in doing *that*. Meaning the color certainly did not consist in looking hard at the color, nor in saying to yourself "What a great

5. See *Zettel*, paras. 1–2 and paras. 38–50; *Investigations*, paras. 631–693.
6. *Investigations*, para. 674.

color!" Those things could have occurred and yet you might not have meant the color; and likewise you might have meant the color without their occurrence.

At this stage our thinking is likely to take a peculiar turn. We meant the color; yet we cannot specify anything we did or anything that occurred, which can be identified with meaning the color. So we think: "Meaning the color is just something that occurs in the mind. You cannot say what it is, but you *know* what it is. It is a unique, indescribable mental occurrence. It is something definite but impalpable."

As Wittgenstein remarks, this inclination to think of the mental state of meaning the color as being "impalpable" or "intangible" (*ungreisbar*) is one of the greatest importance.[7] It expresses our idea that mental phenomena are somehow mysterious. Mental acts and states, we feel, are tremendously significant. But we cannot say what they are. Meaning the color just is "a particular mental act." Remembering what you ate for breakfast is "a certain mental experience." Intending to say "So I must leave at ten o'clock" is a perfectly concrete but indescribable mental state. William James produced a splendid expression of this way of thinking:

And has the reader never asked himself what kind of a mental fact is his *intention of saying a thing* before he has said it? It is an entirely definite intention, distinct from all other intentions, an absolutely distinct state of consciousness, therefore; and yet how much of it consists of definite sensorial images, either of words or of things? Hardly anything! Linger, and the words and things come into mind; the anticipatory intention, the divination is there no more. But as the words that replace it arrive, it welcomes them successively and calls them right if they agree with it, it rejects them and calls them wrong if they do not. It has therefore a nature of its own of the most positive sort, and yet what can we say about it without using words that belong to the later mental facts that replace it? The intention *to-say-so-and-so* is the only name it can receive.[8]

7. Ibid., para. 608; paras. 173–175. Also see Wittgenstein, *Blue and Brown Books* (Oxford, 1958), pp. 158–162.

8. William James, *The Principles of Psychology* (New York, 1890), 253. The same viewpoint appears in the programs and conclusions of the Würzburg psychologists. They wanted to find out what happens when one makes a judgment. They held that

As James saw it, when we think and speak, intending this or that by our words, there is a continuous flow of feelings and experiences, which comprise the thinking and meaning. When we intend a word in a certain sense, the intention is a definite state of consciousness. We are aware of it. James gave the following example:

> Again, when we use a common noun, such as *man*, in a universal sense, as signifying all possible men, we are fully aware of this intention on our part, and distinguish it carefully from our intention when we mean a certain group of men, or a solitary individual before us. . . . It casts its influence over the whole of the sentence, both before and after the spot in which the word *man* is used.[9]

James thought that there were subtle differences in the way the word "man" feels, when you use it in different senses, and that these different feelings spread themselves throughout the sentences in which the word occurs: "We all of us have the permanent con-

---

"a strict experimental procedure must be used. A number of observers must be caused to make judgments under standard, controllable conditions, and a careful record made of what takes place in their consciousness. Thus we shall find out what a judgment is" (George Humphrey, *Thinking* [New York, 1951], p. 34). The results of experimentally controlled introspection were initially a shock to the Würzburg group. Judgments are "recognized as such" but "with nothing in consciousness to indicate why they are judgments!" (ibid., p 35). No "psychological criterion" of judgment was found; but there were found certain "facts of consciousness, whose content either escapes further characterization altogether, or proves accessible to such characterization only with difficulty" (ibid., p. 36). "Impalpable," "unanalysable," awarenesses, tendencies, and meanings were noted. "The impalpably given content of the awareness is often elusive" (ibid., p. 48).

A member of the group tackled the "fundamental" question stated in the following equivalent formulations: "What happens when people think?" (ibid., p. 55); "What is our actual experience when we think?"; "What are our experiences when we think, considered purely as modifications of consciousness and apart from their context?" (ibid., pp. 56, 57). The findings of introspection were as follows: "Our thinking consists essentially of a specific process which must be considered to constitute a fresh mental category." "A thought is not the sum of a number of images. It is a true, unanalysable unity." "The thought of something is . . . an irreducible fact of experience" (ibid., p 58).

The Würzburg investigators believed themselves to have discovered that when you think or judge there occurs some "unique," "unanalysable," "impalpable" experience.

9. James, I, 256.

sciousness of whither our thought is going. It is a feeling like any other, a feeling of what thoughts are next to arise, before they have arisen." [10] But is there any truth in James' notion? If you reflect on actual conversations in which you say the word "man"—sometimes meaning all men, sometimes this or that man, sometimes some man or other, sometimes using the word as an exclamation ("Man!")—you will not detect those subtly different feelings that are supposed to go with the different intentions.

James was trying to do what all of us should like to do, namely, to say what went on in us when we uttered a word and meant it in a certain sense. But (like the Würzburg psychologist) we do not succeed. So we are inclined to say that what went on is impalpable, intangible. We cannot get hold of it! We should like to be able to say exactly what intending the letter for the Tom in Omaha *is*. But we cannot do it. We cannot identify it with having an image of the Omaha Tom, nor with saying "Omaha" silently to oneself, nor with any feeling. We should like to say, "I pointed at him in my mind." [11] At the same time, we are embarrassed to say this. For how can one *point at him in one's mind?* So we are inclined to give up all comparisons and characterizations, and to say that intending the letter for the Tom in Omaha just is "a particular mental act." Wittgenstein observes that when we speak in this way, part of the force of the word "mental" is to indicate that "we mustn't expect to understand how these things work." [12] The word "mental" serves here to signify what is mysterious, inexplicable, occult.

Let us see if we can do anything to dispel the mysteriousness. Perhaps we cannot explain what intending the letter for the Tom of Omaha *consists in;* but we can say what *connects* the letter with the one Tom rather than the other. The connection would be different in different cases. Suppose that the Tom in Omaha was a garage

10. Ibid., pp. 255–256. See also p. 472: "This added consciousness is an absolutely positive sort of feeling transforming what would otherwise be mere noise or vision into something *understood;* and determining the sequel of my thinking, the later words and images, in a perfectly definite way."

11. Cf. *Zettel*, para. 12.   12. *Blue and Brown Books*, p. 39.

mechanic and the one in Buffalo was a dentist, and I knew this. I announced to my wife that I was going to write to Tom; and then I said, "I wonder whether he still works in that same garage." In this way I connected the letter with the Omaha Tom. My remark occurred *before* the letter was written. But also I might have made it *during* the writing of the letter, and also *after* the writing. Or (another case) in the previous hour we had talked about Tom and had remarked that he still lives in Omaha, and I had declared that I was going to write to him. Or (another case) after completing the letter I wrote on the envelope the address of the Tom of Omaha. Or (still another case) I said, while writing, "This letter is to Tom in Omaha." In these various ways the letter could have got connected with him.

Or it could be that I was thinking of the Omaha Tom as I wrote; or that I saw him in my mind as I wrote. These facts would connect my letter with him no less, and *no more*, than would my writing the Omaha address on the envelope or my saying aloud that I was writing to the one in Omaha. My thoughts may connect my letter with him, but not in a way that is superior to the way my words do it.[13]

Or it could have been that none of the previously mentioned phenomena occurred, but it was true that *if* I had been asked I *should have* answered that I was writing to the Tom in Omaha. Although this fact is only conditional, still it connects the letter with him.[14]

I have spoken of certain facts as "connecting" the letter with the Tom of Omaha. Is this connection an *entailment?* This is a question that has previously perplexed me and a good many other philosophers. It might be called "the problem of criteria." From the fact that I said "I wonder whether he still works in that same garage," or that I said "This letter is to Tom in Omaha," or that I was thinking of the Omaha Tom as I wrote, does it follow, with logical

13. Cf. *Zettel*, para. 9.   14. Cf. *Investigations*, para. 684.

necessity, that I meant the letter for him? The answer is, no. Certainly not.

We want to ask: "But how then can such facts *connect* the letter with him if they do not provide an entailment?" The following analogy may be helpful. Suppose we draw two schematic human faces, whose only difference is that in one the mouth is a horizontal straight line, in the other a line that curves upward at both ends. Consequently the second is a smiling face, but the first is not. It is right to say that the curved mouth line "makes" the one a smiling face, or "gives" it a smiling aspect. "It makes the difference." But there is no entailment. Certainly that mouth would not make just any face a smiling face. The other lines could be changed, or new lines added, in such a way that the face would no longer smile. With the mouth line unchanged the expression might become, for example, a sneer, or a leer, or a look of ferocity. Wittgenstein remarks how we sometimes say that what gives a certain person's face a friendly look are his friendly eyes. But: "It does not follow from the fact that there is what we call a friendly and an unfriendly expression of the eye that there must be a difference between the eye of a friendly and the eye of an unfriendly face." [15] We are tempted to think that a certain feature cannot *make* a face look friendly, if some other feature could destroy that effect. But this is not so. "It is true that other traits in this face could take away the friendly character of this eye, and yet in this face it is the eye which is the outstanding friendly feature." [16] Furthermore, even if we did not alter or add anything to the smiling schematic face, we could spin a story around it which would alter our way of seeing it. We could see the expression as gloating, or as a forced but unsuccessful attempt at a smile, and so on. We will see the fact differently, depending on the human context that we imagine. [17]

These comparisons are intended to suggest that something I do, say, or think, can have the character of being the "outstanding" fea-

15. *Blue and Brown Books*, p. 145.   16. Ibid., p. 146.
17. Cf. *Investigations*, para. 539.

ture of a situation in which I am writing a letter—in the sense that we can rightly say that this feature *makes* my letter a letter to the Tom of Omaha, or that it *connects the letter with him. But they are also meant to show that this will be so only in a certain context. Change the latter in various ways, then the same words, thoughts, or actions would not* make it a letter to him.

Nor can we produce an entailment by conjoining some outstanding feature with *all* of the relevant circumstances. There is no "all" here. Our language does not contain closed rules of that sort.

Something I say or do will be used by other people as a criterion of my meaning my letter for the Omaha Tom. That is how they will respond and judge. But the connection between a criterion and what it is a criterion of is not "certified by logic." (I will come back to this point later.)

Let us return to the example of your pointing toward a flower and exclaiming "Look!" where what you meant, what you were pointing at, was its color. How would this differ from a case in which you meant its shape, or its size, or its species? The way to get the answer is to imagine various surroundings for the act of pointing. Suppose that you and your companion belong to a group that is studying colors in nature. The leader of the group has just given a lecture on "pure" colors, and now the group is on a walk through the woods for the purpose of observing examples of pure natural colors. Each member is to keep a record of the examples he spots. You point at a flower and say "Look!" You and your companion write in your notebooks: "Saw a pure yellow near a large sycamore tree."

The feeling of mystery has vanished. In those circumstances you meant the color. If the circumstances had been different in certain ways you would have meant something else. We are tempted to think that your meaning the color must have been something that went on in your mind. But it might be that what went on in your mind or thoughts had *nothing* to do with what you meant. You might have thought to yourself, "What a *huge* flower!"; but still (in our example) it was its color you meant when you pointed, and not its size. Or you might have been impressed by its shape, following the outline of it with your eyes. But given the other circumstances as described, it still would not have been the shape you meant when you spoke and pointed.

We begin to see that it was the pattern of circumstances that gave your act of pointing its specific meaning. We have an inclination to think that your meaning the color was an event that accompanied the pointing but was hidden underneath it. We thought we had to go *down* and *in* to find it. That is the idea we have when, puzzled about how we are able to mean something, we say that it is a "mental" event or act. Wittgenstein says to us: "Do not make that move! You are going in the wrong direction."

Instead of looking *inside* ourselves we should be looking *around* us, at the context in which our words and pointing are located. We should be searching horizontally instead of vertically. This temptation to look in the wrong direction besets us whenever we are perplexed about the concepts of mind. Wittgenstein's admonition applies to all of them. He says, for example, that you should not think of the sudden understanding of some problem as a "mental" occurrence.[18] Why not? Not because this is *false*. Your thinking here is too nebulous to be false. The reason for avoiding that way of speaking is that it confuses you.[19] It leads you astray. It throws you off the track. It makes you want to search in the wrong place for the way out of your perplexity. You become a fly in a flybottle.[20]

As Wittgenstein remarks, he does not *deny* that remembering an engagement, for example, is an "inner event." How could he? *What* event? No one can say. He describes his own aim in this way:

18. Ibid., para. 154; *Zettel*, para. 446. In talking about our philosophical inclinations Wittgenstein uses the expressions "mental occurrence" (*seelischer Vorgang*) and "inner occurrence" (*innerer Vorgang*) interchangeably. This is not because whatever is "mental" is in fact "inner" (whatever that might mean), but because that is how we think of it. We have the idea that suddenly understanding the solution of a problem, or suddenly remembering an engagement, or meaning the color when you pointed, are occurrences "in the mind" or "inside" us.

19. Ibid.   20. *Investigations*, para. 309.

"The impression that we wanted to deny something arises from the fact that we turn against the picture of the 'inner event.' What we deny is that the picture of the inner event gives us the correct idea of the use of the word 'remember.' We say that this picture with its ramifications stands in the way of our seeing the use of the word as it is." [21] Wittgenstein is rejecting a *picture*, and the mode of expression that conveys that picture. He does not hold that remembering is *not* an "inner" or "mental" event. Insofar as there is any concrete meaning in saying "The mental event of remembering the picnic has just taken place in me," it comes to the same as saying "I have just remembered the picnic." Thus, "To deny the mental event would mean to deny the remembering," [22] which would be absurd.

The picture of remembering, or meaning, or thinking, as being a "mental event," an "inner occurrence," "something that happens in the mind," has a hypnotic effect. It prevents a philosopher from observing the situations and activities, the contexts, to which the words "remember," "mean," "think," etc., belong and which give them all the significance they have. The picture makes it seem that such observation is really irrelevant, because it can only show us in what cases we *say* of someone, "He meant the color" or "He meant the shape"—(as if that could be disregarded). This picture of meaning, remembering, etc., as "something I do in my mind" turns us away from the only study that could give us a clear view of our concepts. Thus it is not *just* a picture but a harmful influence.

In our puzzlement about mind there is an even more basic picture that forces itself on us and seems to define our problem. The picture is that meaning (or intending, remembering, thinking, joy, or anger) must be either something *inner* or something *outer*. The problem becomes one of determining which it is. That it is one *or* the other is self-evident, we think.

But whichever horn of this dilemma we choose, there are decisive objections. Joy is often manifested in joyful behavior; but, as Wittgenstein says, "Joy is not joyful behavior." [23] A young

---

21. Ibid., para. 305.   22. Ibid., para. 306.   23. *Zettel*, para. 487.

woman's joyous exclamations, movements, smiles, would not be manifestations of joy if they occurred in quite different circumstances. Instead they could belong to a bitter parody of joy; or they could be symptoms of madness.[24]

This difficulty cannot be remedied by thinking up more complex constructions out of behavior (e.g., stimulus-response functions) in terms of which joy would be defined. The point holds for all of the psychological concepts. When you pointed toward the flower and said "Look!", your meaning its color did not consist in that behavior. Nor did it consist in the conditional fact that *if* the words "Do you mean the color?" had been addressed to you, you would have answered "Yes." As Wittgenstein remarks: " 'Meaning' does not stand for an activity which wholly or partly consists in the outward expressions of meaning." [25] In general, meaning, joy, or remembering cannot be identified with any sequence of behavioral manifestations, nor with any *disposition* to manifest such behavior given certain conditions of stimulation.

These reflections may make us turn away from behaviorism and seize the other horn of the dilemma, which is the idea that meaning, remembering, anger, and joy are *inner* occurrences or states. But nothing of this sort, that we can *specify*, is an adequate candidate. Anger is often characterized by sensations that go with the swelling of the chest or the flaming of the cheeks; but it cannot be identified with such sensations. Meaning your letter for the Tom of Omaha did not consist in your seeing him in your mind, even if this happened.

Realizing this, we are inevitably pushed toward thinking that joy is an unspecifiable inner state, that meaning is an indescribable inner occurrence, and so on. Thus our desire to *identify* the phenomena of mind, together with our idea that they must consist in

24. "A coronation is the picture of pomp and dignity. Cut one minute of this proceeding out of its surroundings: the crown is being placed on the head of the king in his coronation robes. But in different surroundings gold is the cheapest of metals, its gleam is thought vulgar. There the fabric of the robe is cheap to produce. A crown is a parody of a respectable hat. And so on "(*Investigations*, para. 584).

25. *Zettel*, para. 19.

something inner or something outer, carries us by a natural progression to the thought that meaning, remembering, thinking, joy, etc., are, each of them, unspecifiable, indescribable, inner states or events. You feel that you know what meaning or remembering are; you can almost *see* them going on inside you; [26] yet you cannot *say* what they are. You know what they are, but you cannot tell anyone.

Through these stages we are driven to the idea that the phenomena of mind are *inner, indescribable,* and *private.* There is no doubt that this idea gets a much deeper hold on us than does its rival, behaviorism. [27] But it can be seen that it produces intolerable consequences. For if meaning the color were something inner, indescribable, and private (the same being true for meaning the size or the shape), then how could I possibly know that you meant the color of the flower when you pointed and said "Look!"? If you said, on being questioned, "I meant the color," how could I know what you meant by *those words?* How could I learn *which* inner event it is that is supposed to be designated by the phrase "meaning the color"? How could I know whether you and I use that phrase to refer to the same kind of inner event? How, indeed, could the belief that the same kind of thing takes place in you as in me even be intelligible to me? How can I *think* that what goes on in us is the same (or is not the same)? For I am supposed not to be able to *specify how* it is the same. Am I to concentrate on something in myself and then conceive that you have *it?* But what is *it?* Is it my meaning, or my frustration, or possibly my concentration itself? If I cannot say or show in any way what I have picked out (which is the hypothesis), what entitles us to assume that I have picked out anything?—that I have conceived of anything at all in conceiving that you have *it?* Would it matter if you and I picked out *different* inner things (supposing that means something), provided that we agreed in our use of language?

26. *Investigations,* para. 305.
27. This is surely why Wittgenstein devotes far more attention to the idea of the inner than to behaviorism.

The conception of the phenomena of mind as being inner, indescribable, private, leaves us floundering in a quagmire. So where are we to turn? The picture of intending, thinking, joy, etc., as consisting in either something inner or something outer, has let us down. It does not give us any possible solutions. We have reached this impasse because, according to Wittgenstein, we made a fundamental error. We assumed that meaning, joy, remembering, etc., must *consist in something*. And it seemed to us that the something must be either inner or outer. Wittgenstein thinks, however, that it is a mistake to say that your meaning the color *consists in something*.[28] Having said that joy is not "joyful behavior,"[29] he then imagines someone declaring that the word "joy" designates something *inner*, to which he replies: "No. 'Joy' designates nothing at all. Neither inner nor outer."[30]

Of course he is not saying that the word "joy" is meaningless. Its meaning is its use in the language. It is not used to stand for some constellation of behavioral responses. There is no grouping of gestures, movements, utterances, such that we can say: *That* is what joy is. We remarked before that any sequence of such behavior could occur in a context in which it would not be a manifestation of joy, but of something else. So joy is not something *outer*. But if we turn in the other direction and try to identify it with something *inner* we make a hopeless move, since here we do not know what we mean.

A carpenter building a structure sometimes works merely mechanically. But at other times he puts *thought* into his work: he measures, makes tests, considers different possibilities, comes to a decision, rejects this piece of wood, searches for another of the right length, discovers a mistake in the structure, hits upon a solution, expresses satisfaction, and so on. When he is thus putting thought into his work he will normally present a different appearance from when he is working merely mechanically. In the one case there are the activities of measuring, testing, trying; the facial

28. *Zettel*, para. 16: *"Der Irrtum ist zu sagen, Meinen bestehe in etwas."*
29. Ibid., para. 487.   30. Ibid.

expressions, movements, exclamations, which express dissatisfaction, hesitation, searching, finding, or deciding. Little, if any, of this will be present in the other case. But we cannot say that the thinking which is present in the one case but not in the other *is* those activities, facial expressions, movements, and exclamations. Nor yet can we say that the thinking is a stream that flows underneath those manifestations of thinking,[31] any more than we can say that when you read a sentence and understand it, your understanding of it is something that flows along with the reading (which is what William James thought).

I want to say more about the kind of mistake we make when we assume that thinking (meaning, expecting, or remembering, etc.) consists in something; when, as one might say, we seek to *identify* it. Let us consider remembering. Suppose that after driving your car you put the keys in the kitchen drawer. Several hours later someone else wants to drive the car and asks, "Where did you put the keys?" Now imagine the following cases:

(1) Nothing occurs to you: you feel at a loss and also, as it were, guilty. Then you think to yourself: "After I left the car I entered the house by the kitchen door." You have an image of the kitchen and of your hand pulling open the drawer. You say: "I left them in the kitchen drawer."

(2) You say: "Now let me think." You close your eyes but no images come. Nothing occurs to you, and you feel embarrassed. You say to yourself, "Where could I have put them?" Suddenly you exclaim: "The kitchen drawer!"

(3) When the question was addressed to you, you were speaking to another person. Without interrupting your remarks, which were on a different topic, you pointed at the kitchen drawer.

(4) When the question was put to you, you were writing a letter. You got up from your chair, walked into the kitchen, took the keys out of the drawer, and handed them over. But all the while you were turning over in your mind a phrase of the letter.

31. Ibid., paras. 100, 101, 106, 107.

(5) In response to the question you say to yourself, "Why does he want the keys?" Then you say aloud, "I seem to remember putting them in the kitchen drawer, but I am not sure."

(6) Without any hesitation or doubt, or reflection or imagery, you say straight off, "I put them in the kitchen drawer."

In all of these cases we should say that you remembered where you put the keys. We ought to be struck by the variety exhibited in these examples. (And, of course, many more examples, exhibiting still other differences, could be provided.) In one case you *tried* to remember; in another case not. In one case you were preoccupied with other matters as you indicated the whereabouts of the keys; in another case not. Your actions were different in these examples. In one case there were relevant thoughts and imagery; in another not. In one case you knew the answer immediately; in another not. And the degree of your confidence differed in these examples.

We will agree that your remembering where you put the keys did not consist in your having an image of the drawer, nor in your pointing at it, nor in your feeling confident that you put them there, and so on. So what did the remembering consist in? As Wittgenstein remarks, "No answer comes." [32]

Here our philosophical thinking reaches a crucial intersection. We can take the familiar path (which is a dead end) of assuming that in addition to the phenomena we described in each case, there was the remembering itself (for it is true that you remembered); and since the remembering cannot be identified with any of those phenomena, it must be something intangible and hidden. Or, we can shift our whole viewpoint and say: "No. Our examples of remembering were not incompletely described. We gave an accurate account of what happened when you remembered. There was not some further occurrence which was the remembering itself." If we go in this new direction we will be overcoming the inclination to think there *must* be a mental occurrence of remembering in addition to the words, gestures, or actions by which remembering is

32. *Investigations*, para. 678, and also para. 175; *Zettel*, para. 162.

expressed.[33] We shall be ready to acknowledge that the word "remembering" is actually used by us to range over a diversity of events and circumstances that are not united by an essential nature of remembering. In understanding this we shall be freeing ourselves from the obsessive desire to *penetrate the phenomena*.

Wittgenstein remarks that although we learn the use of the word "remember" ("think," or "mean") we do not learn to *describe* its use.[34] We are not prepared for that task. Furthermore, we tend to have a false picture of the use of the word. "We expect a smooth, regular contour and what we get to see is ragged." [35] What we find is that an irregular multitude of phenomena and situations are called "remembering."

Why do we form the false picture at all? Partly because *the same word*, "remembering," is used throughout. Yet, as Wittgenstein says, it ought not to be expected that this word "should have a unified employment; we should rather expect the opposite." [36] Why should we expect the opposite? Because we were not taught to use the word by means of a precise definition, nor by any definition at all. We heard the word used in this case and that case. And then we ourselves went on to use it in other cases—the same as everyone else does. We were not shown the "essential nature" of remembering, whatever that might be.

It is the same as with the words "tree" or "dog." Why should a greyhound and a Pekinese both be called "dogs"? They are so different. Is it *reasonable* to call them both dogs? We can easily imagine people who would think there was too much of a gap here. Could we prove them wrong?

Consider the diversity in the applications of the word "remembering." Remembering a word is different from remembering a face; and remembering a sensation is still different. Remembering

33. "I have been trying in all this to remove the temptation to think that there 'must be' what is called a mental process of thinking, hoping, wishing, believing, etc., independent of the process of expressing a thought, a hope, a wish, etc." (*Blue and Brown Books*, p. 41).

34. *Zettel*, para. 114.   35. Ibid., para. 111.   36. Ibid., para. 112.

your uncle is different from remembering that you have an uncle. Remembering to fix the radiator is different from remembering how to fix it. Even with a single locution, such as "remembering where one put the keys," there is, as we saw, a striking diversity of phenomena. In one case there was uncertainty, anxiety, concentration, putting questions to oneself, and then suddenly saying where one put the keys. In another case none of this happened; one just walked over to the drawer and pulled out the keys, all the while engaged in a discussion of some other topic. Is it *justifiable* to apply the same word to these cases?

Whether it is justifiable or not, we do it. What is the explanation of our applying the same word over such a wide range of heterogeneous cases? Is it because we know the meaning of the word? Does its meaning serve as our guide? This is a foolish way of thinking; for what is it to know the meaning of the word other than to apply it here, and to refuse to apply it there, and to be in doubt in some other cases, just like everyone else? Our "knowing the meaning of the word" is nothing other than our applying it, in substantial agreement with others, to that astonishing variety of contexts and reactions. Therefore, it cannot explain or justify this fact.

Wittgenstein says that his philosophical observations are "remarks on the natural history of human beings." [37] It would be difficult to exaggerate the significance of that comment. It is often said that Wittgenstein's work belongs to "linguistic philosophy"—that he "talks about words." True enough. But he is trying to get his reader to think of how the words are tied up with human life, with patterns of response, in thought and action. His conceptual studies are a kind of anthropology. His descriptions of the human forms of life on which our concepts are based make us aware of the kind of creature we are.

We have been noting an illustration of this. It is a striking fact, although always under our noses,[38] that from an instruction in the application of a word, employing only a few examples and frag-

37. *Investigations*, para. 415; cf. para. 25.   38. Cf. ibid., para. 129.

mentary explanations, we go on to apply that word in new case after new case, the new cases differing in numerous ways from the examples we were originally given, yet we largely *agree!* It would seem that from the original instruction we could branch out in an indefinitely large number of paths, each of us going a different way. And it is true that we *could*. But we do not. The fact that we do not, the fact that almost everyone goes on in approximately the same way, is a feature of the natural history of human beings.

We are tempted to think that our common agreement in the use of the word "remembering," for example, must have an *explanation*. We feel that the explanation must be that we perceived, intuited, guessed, or somehow abstracted the *essence* of remembering, the *meaning* of the word, from the examples that were presented to us: we grasped the universal. As if in being given the examples we were given at the same time something deeper, something that went beyond the examples.[39] But this "explanation" is a pretence since we cannot say what the supposed essence of remembering is.

When a person learns to use a word, there is, as Wittgenstein says, no wheel that he catches hold of that, once grasped, carries him on automatically.[40] That is how we tend to think of it: as if there were a commmon structure of remembering that we abstract from the examples we encounter, and once we have laid hold of it we are drawn along from case to case. Yet not only is there no common structure of remembering, but even if there were it would not help, because we should have to apply *it* in the right way to new cases. Whether it came to us as an image, or a formula, or a definition, or an intuition, or a rule—there would be the *possibility* that different people would apply it *differently*. In whatever form it was presented to us it would be open to different interpretations. There can be no way of taking it that is, so to speak, logically forced on us. There is no "logical compulsion."

Thus even if there were an essential nature of remembering to be grasped, this would not get us out of the predicament we feel we

39. Cf. ibid., para. 71.   40. *Zettel*, para. 304.

are in (which is really no predicament at all). We thought we required an *explanation* of why we generally agree in our employment of the word "remembering," and we imagined that the explanation might be that all of us got hold of the one essence of remembering. We see now that even if this were true, we would still be confronted by the same difficulty. For we should now need an explanation of the fact of our agreeing on how to read that essence— agreeing on what *it* requires us to say in each new situation. And is this not the very sort of fact we were wanting to explain? [41]

It may be useful at this point to try again to prevent a misunderstanding of Wittgenstein's emphasis on the significance of the *context* (the surroundings, the pattern of circumstances, the "language-game") in determining the application of our concepts of thinking, remembering, etc. Someone might think that Wittgenstein wants to substitute definitions in terms of contexts for definitions in terms of outer behavior or of inner states. If this could be done it might make us happy, for then we could think of ourselves as employing the mental terms in accordance with iron rules of context. We could suppose that somehow all of us assimilate the same linguistic rules and that the rules we thus absorb thereafter control our subsequent applications of the mental terms. But one flaw in this picture is that there are no inflexible rules of context. Circumstances are immensely relevant to what we shall say; but they provide neither definitions nor entailments. Given a context in which we shall say that the person who pointed and said "Look!" meant the color of the flower, it does not logically follow from a description of the context that this is what he meant. For that context could be placed in a still wider context, such that any impression of his having meant the color would be removed. We cannot reach a point where

41. This is the point of *Investigations*, para. 86, and *Blue and Brown Books*, pp. 90–91. We are given a column of names and a column of pictures, and a column of horizontal arrows showing how the names are to be correlated with the pictures. But might not a second column of arrows, slanted ones, show how the horizontal arrows are to be read? And might there not be still a third column of arrows, slanted differently, which show how the arrows of the second column are to be taken? *And so on?*

we can rightly say that no conceivable addition of further circumstances would make any difference. We do not circumscribe our concepts like that.[42]

Another thing wrong with picturing fixed rules of context is that it is just another manuever by which we try to explain to ourselves how *common agreement* in the application of language is possible. It is a fact that when human beings are given a few examples of the application of a word they go on to make further applications in agreement with one another. They do not branch out in innumerable directions. In short, there is a *normal response* to the training. Wittgenstein calls this a "proto-phenomenon" (*Urphäenomen*). He says: "Our mistake is to look for an explanation where we should see what happens as a 'proto-phenomenon'." [43] Why is it a mistake to seek an explanation? Because the *kind* of fact we are trying to explain (namely, the occurrence of a normal response) will reappear in our supposed explanation. We shall have achieved nothing. We deceive ourselves into thinking we have increased our understanding.

An example of a typically futile exercise in explanation is Wolfgang Köhler's attempt to explain so-called "successive comparison." If I hear a note struck on the piano, and five seconds later hear another one, and the second one seems louder or is heard as louder, this would be an instance of "successive comparison." Or if I lift a weight and then another, and the second feels heavier (or lighter) than the first. Or if I report that a color I see now is brighter (or darker) than one I saw a minute ago. And so on. Köhler says: "In successive comparison we recognize a relation which obtains between two objects given at different times. It stands to reason that there can be no relation, unless there be at least two terms of which the relation is predicated. At the time of

---

42. "If someone were to draw a sharp boundary I could not acknowledge it as the one that I too always wanted to draw, or had drawn in my mind. For I did not want to draw one at all" (*Investigations*, para. 76).

43. Ibid., para. 654.

comparing the subject must therefore have two such terms." [44] But Köhler finds a puzzle here. For the first sound has vanished into the past—so how can I compare the second sound with *it?* Or how can I compare color A and color B, when I see B but not A? There must be some *explanation* of how I do it, or of what I do. The explanation will, of course, consist in postulating some *surrogate* for the "missing" term.

Köhler indicates that an acceptable surrogate would be a memory image of the first sound (or weight, or color). We could then compare the second sound with our (simultaneous) memory image of the first one. But he finds that this does not actually occur; at least not very often. "When comparing two objects or events which are given successively we do not, as a rule, produce a memory image of the first when the second appears." [45] Furthermore, he says, an actual memory image is usually not "a sufficiently adequate copy of the first impression." If the image is not an adequate copy, then it will not account for the accuracy of the comparison; and it may even "*disturb* the process of comparison." [46]

Let us suppose, however, that there is, in a particular case of successive sounds, a memory image which *is* a "sufficiently adequate" copy of the first sound. Köhler's thinking seems to be that successive comparison would be explained in that case. But would it? After all, the memory image exists *after* the first sound has ceased. So here is a gap to be bridged—the same kind of gap that created the original problem. The gap is between the *image* of the first sound and the first sound itself. The thought that the image is (or is not) a "sufficiently adequate" copy of the first sound implies a *comparison*. The first term of this comparison has ceased to exist. By Köhler's reasoning a surrogate is required for it. So the first surrogate of the first sound must be compared with a *second* surrogate of the first sound. But there will be a temporal gap between the sec-

44. Wolfgang Köhler, *The Place of Value in a World of Facts* (New York, 1938), pp. 269–270.

45. Ibid., p. 270.   46. Ibid.

ond surrogate and the first sound itself. This required a *third* surrogate of the latter. And so on. This regress cannot be terminated!

Köhler failed to notice that the supposed problem of successive comparison is presented just as much by the temporal separation between the surrogate image and the first sound as by the temporal separation between the second sound and the first sound. This problem *could not* be solved by substituting a memory image for the first sound.

Let us return to Köhler's presentation. There may occur, he says, "a genuine judgment of comparison even in the absence of a memory image." [47] But if the second sound (or the "impression" of it) "is not referred to such an image, it is nevertheless clearly referred to *something*." [48] What is this "something"? Köhler believes that it must be some state or process of the central nervous system. He thinks that, first of all, some neural process was correlated with one's "impression" of the first sound. This neural process produced, in turn, a memory trace. The trace is a neural state or process that persists after the first sound is no longer heard.

The trace, says Köhler, "must be a more or less adequate representative" of the neural process that produced the trace and was correlated with the impression of the first sound.[49] (It would appear that the trace also "represents" the impression of the first sound, and also the first sound itself.) Now notice what Köhler says: "In successive comparison this trace is then the thing 'beyond' with which the present event is felt to be in reference." [50]

By "the present event" he means either the second sound or (possibly) the impression of it. To say that either one is "felt to be in reference" with the brain trace *should* mean that one compares the second sound (or the impression of it) with the brain trace that "represents" the first sound (or represents the impression of the first sound, or represents the neural process that was correlated with that impression). But what an absurd result! In what dimension does one compare them? Certainly not in the dimension of

47. Ibid., p. 271.   48. Ibid.   49. Ibid., p. 272.   50. Ibid.

loudness. It would be nonsense to say that one heard the second sound as louder than *the brain trace* of the first sound. But loudness was the dimension of comparison we started with. One heard the second sound as louder than the first. This perplexed Köhler, because the first sound did not exist when the second occurred: so *what* did one compare the second one with? [51]

The heart of the matter is that Köhler finds the idea of *successive* comparison unintelligible; so he wants to replace it with *simultaneous* comparison. The second sound is going to be compared with some *coexisting* thing. It should be clear, however, that no solution along those lines can work. For the coexisting thing must be something that can be compared with the second sound in loudness, that being the dimension of the original comparison. The only sort of thing that could be compared with the second sound in loudness would be a *sound*. But if we proposed a sound as the surrogate for the first sound—and, of course, a sound that *coexists* with the second sound—then we should have lost hold of the problem entirely. For how could substituting simultaneous for successive sounds remove one's puzzlement over the comparison of *successive* sounds? And if simultaneous sounds would be irrelevant to the problem so would simultaneous anything.

We started out from the prosaic fact that a person hears the second of two sounds as louder. Köhler's puzzle is how the second sound can refer (or be referred) to something that does not exist. He thinks to solve this puzzle by supposing that the second sound refers (or is referred) to something that coexists with it, namely, a neural trace of the first sound. He could not, however, believe this to be any kind of solution unless he thought that the neural trace "represents" the first sound. As he says, the trace of the first sound "must be sufficiently representative of its loudness to make the second tone emerge with the *right* direction." [52] "Emerging with the right direction" here means being heard as louder than the first

---

51. This is a special form of the problem, How can one *think of* what is not the case? See *Investigations*, paras. 446–448; *Zettel*, para. 69.

52. Wolfgang Köhler, *Gestalt Psychology* (New York, 2nd ed., 1947), p. 251.

sound. But if it was a problem how the second sound could *refer* to something that no longer exists, it is equally a problem how the neural trace could *represent* something that no longer exists. In saying that the trace *represents* "more or less adequately" either the neural process that established it, or the first sound, or the impression of the first sound, or all three, Köhler is thereby *comparing* (or *referring*) the trace to something that no longer exists. He is doing the very thing that, on his own account, it is impossible to do.

In this attempt to "explain" the hearing of the second sound as louder, the explanation generates the same difficulty it was supposed to remove. Whatever the nature of the surrogate for the first sound, it cannot do its job unless it represents, or stands for, or is somehow referred to the first sound. But that is the supposed crux—something present referred to something absent!

I offer Köhler's problem of successive comparison merely as an illustration of a self-defeating philosophical explanation. A staple of human life (successive comparison) is going to be explained by means of some mental or physical intermediary (a memory image or a neural trace). It turns out (not surprisingly) that the problem to be solved reappears in the solution. So we have gotten exactly nowhere. But there was *no need* to get anywhere! There is no conceptual difficulty inherent to successive comparison. It seems perplexing only if one is dominated by the unjustified notion that *simultaneous* comparison (side by side!) is the *paradigm* of comparison, and that every kind of comparing must somehow be reduced to that. The fact of our hearing one sound as louder than a previous one does not stand in need of some general explanation. This is a natural human power. It is an *Urphäenomen*. It is not clear what "explaining" it could *mean*. Explanations come to an end somewhere, and where should they terminate if not in something as primitive as this?

The phenomena of successive comparison exemplify a part of our common agreement in the application of terms such as "louder," "brighter," and "longer." The feeling that we must explain these phenomena, by postulating some intermediary thing (mental or physical), is an illustration of what Wittgenstein calls "a general disease of thinking." [53] We insist on assuming some intermediary state or process, when it should be evident that it will present us with the same kind of difficulty that was originally felt to be a problem. It is no exaggeration to call the intellectual striving that persists in erecting these self-defeating structures a "disease" of thinking.

On Wittgenstein's view, philosophy should try neither to *identify* nor to *explain* the phenomena of mind. What should it do then? It should *describe language*. It should remind us of what we say. It should bring to mind how we actually use the mental terms that confuse us philosophically. This undertaking is called by Wittgenstein "describing *grammar*." In his view, the purpose of a particular description of grammar will be to remove a particular puzzle. Since there is no limit to what can confuse and puzzle us about the use of an expression, there cannot be a "complete" description of its grammar.

In philosophical studies of grammar we pay attention to our own use of our own language. We study something that is already in our possession. Nothing new is to be found out, but only some old things recalled. As early as 1931, Wittgenstein put this point by saying, "In philosophy one cannot discover anything." [54] In the *Investigations* he expresses it this way: "Everything lies open to view; nothing is hidden." [55]

The title of this paper might have suggested to someone that I was going to set forth Wittgenstein's views on the nature of mental phenomena—on what remembering is, and how it works; and the same for imagining, meaning, and so on. Not at all! Our assumption that there is *a nature of remembering* (or of meaning, thinking, comparing, etc.) to be found out, to be identified or explained, either by philosophy or by science, is the worst mistake we make in

53. See *Blue and Brown Books*, p. 143; cf., p. 130.
54. *Ludwig Wittgenstein und der Wiener Kreis* (Oxford, 1967), notes by Frederick Waismann, ed. B. F. McGuinness, p. 183.
55. *Investigations*, para. 126 and para. 435.

the philosophy of mind. Our whole inquiry gets started off on a false track. It is in this light that I read the following remarks by Wittgenstein:

> How does the philosophical problem about mental processes and states and about behaviourism arise?—The first step is the one that altogether escapes notice. We talk of processes and states and leave their nature undecided. Sometime perhaps we shall know more about them—we think. But that is just what commits us to a particular way of looking at the matter. For we have a definite concept of what it means to learn to know a process better. (The decisive movement in the conjuring trick has been made, and it was the very one that we thought quite innocent.) [56]

> We start off by saying to ourselves: "What is remembering? What is the process of remembering? What takes place when one remembers?" And already we have gone wrong! [57]

56. Ibid., para. 308.

57. It gives me pleasure to acknowledge indebtedness to my friend and former colleague, Bruce Goldberg. In numerous discussions and written communications he has invigorated and shaped my thinking about Wittgenstein.

7 | The Myth of Cognitive Processes and Structures

When philosophers and psychologists speak of "cognitive processes" and "cognitive structures," it is not clear what they are talking about. "Cognition" is an esoteric term; but that is not the main difficulty. If we switch to more humble words of everyday language, such as "memory" or "thinking," the talk of "processes" and "structures" remains obscure. This becomes evident if we reflect on such a question as, "What is the process of remembering?" When asked by a philosopher or psychologist, this question assumes that whenever a person remembers something there is a process of remembering. Consideration of a few examples shows that this is not so. Sometimes we go through a process of *trying* to remember. Suppose that you cannot locate your briefcase. You remember that you were carrying it when you left your office. You review in your mind, or aloud, your itinerary on the way home. "I walked to the bank and cashed a check. Did I have the briefcase when I left the bank? I'm not sure. I then went to the bookstore and bought an atlas. Now I know that I *did* take the briefcase into the bookstore, for I remember putting it down when I paid the cashier. And also I remember now that I had the atlas in one hand and my umbrella in the other when I left the store. So I left it in the bookstore." While saying or thinking these things you may have had feelings of anxiety; images of the streets, the bank, and the store may have passed swiftly through your mind; finally, when the solution came, you may have had a feeling of relief as if a weight had been lifted from you.

Perhaps there would be no harm in calling this combination of utterances, thoughts, images, and feelings, a "process of remembering." We see at once, however, that in a vast number of cases of memory there is *no* process of remembering, in this sense. We are told to fetch the pliers, and without any effort or trying we remember where we left them. We want a clean shirt, and we go to the right drawer without previously ransacking our mind as to which drawer it is. When asked the way to the museum or the name of a novel we read last week, we often give prompt, confident answers. Thus, in the clearest sense of the words, a "process of remembering" occurs only *sometimes* when we remember.

The same would be true of a "process of pattern recognition." More often than not there is no process, just as when one recognizes a friend on the street there is usually no process of recognition. You see his face in the crowd; you smile at him and say "Hi, John." You do not think, "Now where have I seen that face before?"

There is a real difficulty, therefore, in understanding what a psychologist is talking about when he says, for example, that he wants to explain "the process of pattern recognition" or to construct a model for it. In recognizing patterns, shapes, colors, and people there is usually, or often, no *process* of recognition. So *what* is the model a model of?

I suggest that the assumption that whenever one recognizes something there is a process of recognition has a purely philosophical origin. The assumption arises in the following way: we consider an ordinary example of recognition, such as recognizing a friend in a crowd. We reflect on what happened: you smiled at him and said "Hi, John." We then think, "Surely your recognition did not *consist* in that: for you could smile at someone and say those words but not recognize him." True. "So then something else must have occurred; and *it* was the act or process of recognition." But this is a fallacious inference. Although your recognition of your friend cannot be equated with your smiling at him and greeting him, it does not follow that it is identical with *some other event* that occurred when you recognized him. The feeling that it must be leads us to think that the process of recognition is *hidden*. We are not quite sure whether it is a *mental* process or a *brain* process; but if we keep the research going, we shall find out someday, we hope.

The kind of muddle we get into here is described with great acuteness by Wittgenstein. One of his familiar examples is that of someone's suddenly understanding how to continue a numerical series of which he has been shown the initial segment.[1] Now, what occurred when he suddenly understood? Various things might have occurred. He might have thought of a formula that fitted the initial segment, and exclaimed, "I know how it goes." Or instead of a formula, he might have noticed the series of differences, and cried, "I've got it." Or perhaps he did not think of a formula, or of the series of differences, but simply continued the series a few more places, thinking to himself, "This is easy." In these cases there might, or might not, have been initial feelings of tension and subsequent feelings of relief.

But apparently these various descriptions of what might have occurred have not specified what the sudden understanding *itself* was; for a person could think of that formula, or of the series of differences, or continue the initial segment a few places, but still not understand the series. So we think that the essential thing has not yet been brought to light. As Wittgenstein says, "We are trying to get hold of the mental process of understanding which seems to be hidden behind those coarser and therefore more readily visible accompaniments."[2]

The predicament is typical of the attempts of philosophers and psychologists to "analyze" or "explain" the concepts of mind, such as thinking, recognizing, perceiving, meaning, intending, remembering, and problem solving. The feeling that we are dealing with hidden processes gives rise to theories and models. It fosters the desire "to reach a deeper analysis of the phenomena." We feel that when a person recognizes something, in addition to the various

1. Wittgenstein, *Philosophical Investigations*, paras. 151–155.
2. Ibid., para. 153.

manifestations or characteristic accompaniments of recognition, something must go on inside. This is the "inner process" of recognition.

The mistake here is easy to state but profoundly difficult to grasp. Recognizing someone is not an act or process, over and above, or behind, the expression of recognition in behavior. But also, of course, it is not that behavior. As we said, your recognizing John in the crowd cannot be identified with your smiling at him and saying "Hi, John." Imagine an eccentric who smiles at and says "Hi, John," to every tenth person he passes, and who has never seen this John before. Given those facts, his smile and utterance on this occasion would not be an expression of recognition. On the other hand, it is easy to imagine a situation in which such a smile and greeting would be an expression of recognition. Thus, it is the facts, the circumstances surrounding that behavior, that give it the property of expressing recognition. This property is not due to something that goes on inside.

It seems to me that if this point were understood by philosophers and psychologists they would no longer have a motive for constructing theories and models for recognition, memory, thinking, problem solving, understanding, and other "cognitive processes."

I now turn to the notion of "structure," which is so prominent in the thinking of both Piaget and Chomsky. Chomsky has done an impressive job of showing the hopeless inadequacy of a behaviorist account of linguistic competence, in terms of stimulus-response functions. He advocates a "centralist" account. He is struck by the fact that the normal use of language is "innovative," "potentially infinite in scope," "free from the control of detectable stimuli," and "appropriate to a situation." [3]

The central fact to which any significant linguistic theory must address itself is this: a mature speaker can produce a new sentence of his language on the appropriate occasion, and other speakers can understand it immediately, though it is equally new to them. Most of our linguistic experience, both as speakers and hearers, is with new sentences; once we have mas-

3. N. Chomsky, *Language and Mind* (New York, 1968), pp. 10–11.

tered a language, the class of sentences with which we can operate fluently and without difficulty or hesitation is so vast that for all practical purposes (and, obviously, for all theoretical purposes), we can regard it as infinite.[4]

Honesty forces us to admit that we are as far today as Descartes was three centuries ago from understanding just what enables a human to speak in a way that is innovative, free from stimulus control, and also appropriate and coherent.[5]

Chomsky thinks that this normal mastery of language requires that somehow there be *in* a human being "a system of rules," or an "abstract structure," or a "mechanism." This system, structure, or mechanism underlies and explains the multitudinous performances by which the mastery of a language is exhibited. This system is the "grammar" of the language.

The person who has acquired knowledge of a language has internalized a system of rules that relate sound and meaning in a particular way. The linguist constructing a grammar of a language is in effect proposing a hypothesis concerning this internalized system.[6]

It seems clear that we must regard linguistic competence—knowledge of a language—as an abstract system underlying behavior, a system constituted by rules that interact to determine the form and intrinsic meaning of a potentially infinite number of sentences.[7]

It is reasonable to regard the grammar of a language L ideally as a mechanism that provides an enumeration of the sentences of L in something like the way in which a deductive theory gives an enumeration of a set of theorems.[8]

It appears that we recognize a new item as a sentence not because it matches some familiar item in any simple way, but because it is generated by the grammar that each individual has somehow and in some form internalized. And we understand a new sentence, in part, because we are

4. Chomsky, "Current Issues in Linguistic Theory," *The Structure of Language,* ed. J. Fodor and J. J. Katz (Englewood Cliffs, N.J., 1964), p. 50.

5. Chomsky, *Language and Mind,* p. 11.   6. Ibid., p. 23.

7. Ibid., p. 62.

8. Chomsky, "A Review of B. F. Skinner's *Verbal Behavior,*" *The Structure of Language,* p. 576.

somehow capable of determining the process by which this sentence is derived in this grammar.[9]

The child who learns a language has in some sense constructed the grammar for himself on the basis of his observation of sentences and nonsentences (i.e., corrections by the verbal community).[10]

Lenneberg expresses the same viewpoint:

It is generally assumed by linguists—and there are compelling reasons for this—that there must be a finite set of rules that defines all grammatical operations for any given language. Any native speaker will generate sentences that conform to these grammatical rules, and any speaker of the speech community will recognize such sentences as grammatical. We are dealing here with an extremely complex mechanism and one that has never been fully described in purely formal terms for any language (if it had, we could program computers that can "speak" grammatically); and yet, we know that the mechanism must exist for the simple reason that every speaker knows and generally agrees with fellow speakers whether a sentence is grammatical or not.[11]

The philosophical assumption behind this postulation of an "internalized" structure, system, or mechanism is easy to perceive. The assumption is that in speaking a person must be *guided*. There must be something at hand that shows him how to speak, how to put words together grammatically and with coherent sense, and how to recognize a combination of words as being ungrammatical or ambiguous or incoherent. What is being explained is knowledge—both knowing that and knowing how. The presence in him of the structure of the language or of its system of rules is supposed to account for this knowledge—to explain *how* he knows.

The inspiration is the same as for the traditional theory of Ideas. A child is taught the words "chair" or "dog." This is done by means of a comparatively few examples. Then he goes on to apply the words correctly to an indefinite number of new instances of chairs and dogs, which differ in various ways from the original ex-

9. Ibid.   10. Ibid., p. 577.

11. E. H. Lenneberg, "The Capacity for Language Acquisition," *The Structure of Language*, p. 586.

amples. How is he able to do this? How does he know that this new creature is a dog when it is so unlike the dogs he previously encountered? One can feel amazed by this ability, just as Chomsky is amazed when he reflects on the normal ability to produce and understand an unlimited number of sentences never previously encountered. How does one know that this new combination of words is a good English sentence and this other one is not?

The solution provided by the traditional theory is to say that the child has in his mind the *Idea* of a dog. Either he formed ("internalized"?) the Idea by abstraction from the original examples, or else it was in him innately, and was activated by the examples. In either case he possesses the Idea, and he uses it as an object of comparison. He recognizes a new creature as being a dog by comparing it with his Idea; that is how he knows.

One can see this notion at work in Locke. Speaking of "the faculty of retention," he says:

This faculty of laying up and retaining the ideas that are brought into the mind, several other animals seem to have to a great degree, as well as man. For, to pass by other instances, birds learning of turnes, and the endeavours one may observe in them to hit the notes right, put it past doubt with me, that they have perception, and retain ideas in their memories, and use them for patterns. For it seems to me impossible that they should endeavour to conform their voices to notes (as it is plain they do) of which they had no ideas.[12]

The birds must be guided in their whistling by internal patterns of the notes. Otherwise, they could not get the notes right, or even *try* to get them right.

There is an obvious similarity between Locke's reasoning and the reasoning by which Chomsky and Lenneberg support their postulation of a structure, mechanism, system of rules, or internalized grammar. The imagery is somewhat different. In Locke's view the Idea is a model or pattern with which one makes comparisons. With Chomsky and Lenneberg the notion seems to be that the deep

12. Locke, *Essay Concerning Human Understanding*, ed. A. C. Fraser, Bk. II, Ch. 10, Sec. 10.

structure or system is like a set of axioms from which one deduces the sentences one utters.

The criticisms of both views are, or should be, well known. In the first place, this explanation of ability or knowledge is mythological. When I say, "My, that dog is shaggy!" it is not true that I possess a model of a not-so-shaggy dog with which I compare this one. And it is not true that when I carry on an ordinary conversation I deduce my sentences from a set of rules. One might as well say that when I walk along the street, avoiding people, stepping over curbs, etc., my movements are generated by a system of rules. Or that when I chase a rabbit out of the garden my movements are determined by the grammar of chasing a rabbit out of the garden.

It is reassuring to know that there are linguists who reject Chomsky's conception of generative or transformational grammar. Hall, for example, says the following:

As anyone can see by direct observation of ordinary people's normal everyday speech-activity, people simply do not talk according to rules, whether they be aware of the rules' existence or not. There are far too many instances of normal speech which cannot be accounted for by any generative rules at all—which constitute, in fact, all kinds of "violations" of rules—but which cannot be neglected or whose existence cannot be denied on that account.[13]

Hall attacks the notion of Chomsky and Lenneberg that a living language is a calculus: "One cannot establish any set of rules for generating all the possible sentences of a language and none other, because there is no way to determine what is possible and what is not, and because no real language is a closed, well-defined, mathematizable system."[14] It is truly surprising that Chomsky should emphasize the "creative" and "innovative" aspect of normal speech, but at the same time conceive of it as the operation of a deductive system. There are rules in language, but it is wrong to suppose that

13. R. A. Hall, Jr., "Some Recent Developments in American Linguistics," *Neuphilologische Mitteilungen* 70 (1969), 205.

14. Ibid., pp. 207–208.

there is some "complete" set of rules governing our utterances. Wittgenstein offers this analogy:

The regulation of traffic in the streets permits and forbids certain actions on the part of drivers and pedestrians; but it does not attempt to guide the totality of their movements by prescription. And it would be senseless to talk of an "ideal" ordering of traffic which should do that; in the first place we should have no idea what to imagine as this ideal. If someone wants to make traffic regulations stricter on some point or other, that does not mean that he wants to approximate to such an ideal.[15]

The conception of an abstract structure or system controlling the questions, answers, exclamations, orders, oaths, jokes, kidding, etc. of ordinary speech activity is erroneous, not only because that is not how we speak, but also because we do not understand what it would *mean*, what it would be like, for there to be some system or structure generating and determining the flow of intelligible, grammatical speech.

The second criticism of this attempt to explain linguistic competence is that either it leads to an infinite regress, or else it leaves one with the same sort of "mystery" that led to the postulating of a system or structure in the first place. We can see how this works in regard to Locke's Ideas. If we say that the way in which a person knows that something in front of him is a dog is by his seeing that the creature "fits" his Idea of a dog, then we need to ask, "*How* does he know that this is an example of *fitting?*" What guides his judgment here? Does he not need a second-order Idea which shows him what it is like for something to fit an Idea? That is, will he not need a model of *fitting?* But then, surely, a third-order Idea will be required to guide his use of the model of fitting. And so on. An infinite regress has been generated and nothing has been explained.

On the other hand, if we are willing to say that the person *just knows* that the creature he sees fits the first Idea (the Idea of a dog), and no explanation of *this* knowledge is needed—if we are willing to stop here in our search for an explanation of how the man knows that this thing is a dog—then we did not need to start on our search

15. Wittgenstein, *Zettel*, para. 440.

in the first place. We could, just as rationally, have said that the man or child *just knows* (without using any model, pattern or Idea *at all*) that the thing he sees is a dog. We could have said that it is just a normal human capacity (given the initial training) to be able to tell that something is a dog, even if it is quite different from any dog one has previously seen.

That a person knows something cannot be due to his employing an infinite series of models or guides. The explanation of *how* he knows must come to an end. There cannot be an offence to reason here, since the only "alternative" would be the logically impossible performance of consulting an infinite number of models in order to make a single correct identification. Thus, it cannot be a requirement of reason that one should be *guided*.

Obviously this criticism works just as well against the postulation of an abstract structure, or system of rules, or set of principles, that is somehow embedded in a person, and somehow accounts for his linguistic competence, or for his ability to dance the Highland Fling or to whistle Hi-Diddle-Diddle. If the presence of a structure or system is supposed to explain these abilities and performances, then we need to ask, *How* does the person know how to employ the system? Does he have another system that shows him how to use this one? Or does he *just know* how to use it? But if this latter is a rational possibility, then it is also a rational possibility that there is *no* structure or system that accounts for language mastery, or for any repertoire of skills, abilities, or performances. The presence of a guidance system cannot be a general requirement for knowledge.

This point holds for all normal cognitive powers, such as the ability to recognize patterns, or to remember where one parked one's car. The insistence on a structure or mechanism to account for knowledge is a piece of mistaken metaphysics. The error stands out with striking clarity in Lenneberg's remark (previously quoted) in support of the Chomskyan assumption of a system or mechanism of rules in conformity with which a speaker generates sentences: "We know that the mechanism must exist for the simple reason that every speaker knows and generally agrees with fellow speakers whether a sentence is grammatical or not." [16] A mistaken metaphysics lies in this "must." I imagine, however, that Lenneberg is correct in the following remarks:

> Just as we can say with assurance that no man inherits a propensity for French, we can also and with equal confidence say that all men are endowed with an innate propensity for a type of behavior that develops automatically into language and that this propensity is so deeply ingrained that language-like behavior develops even under the most unfavorable conditions of peripheral and even central nervous system impairment. [17]

What is wrong is the assumption that either the languagelike behavior or the subsequent mastery of language must be under the control of underlying systems or structures, schemes or schemas, processes or principles, plans or isomorphic models. Our understanding of human cognitive powers is not advanced by replacing the stimulus-response mythology with a mythology of inner guidance systems.

16. Lenneberg, p. 586.   17. Ibid., p. 589.

8 | Moore and Wittgenstein on the Sense of "I know"

1. In the late 1930's and the early 1940's I was much occupied with the reasoning and conclusions of philosophical skepticism, and greatly impressed by Moore's so-called "defence of common sense." I was anxious to understand the implications for the nature of philosophy of Moore's attitudes and convictions. I was unsympathetic to such typical skeptical views as, for example, that we cannot *see* material things, or that we cannot *know* any empirical proposition to be true. The boldness of Moore's rejection of those views thrilled me. In an essay devoted to Moore, [1] I put forward what came to be called a "linguistic" interpretation of Moore's "defence of common sense," the essence of this interpretation being that Moore was defending not *common sense*, but *ordinary language*, against philosophical arguments and views which imply that innumerable observations of everyday life (such as "I see a squirrel") are really incorrect ways of speaking. [2]

An earlier version of this essay was given as a lecture at The University of Leeds, in May 1974, as part of a commemoration of the 100th anniversary of the birth of G. E. Moore. I am indebted to Sydney Shoemaker for criticisms of that previous version.

1. "Moore and Ordinary Language," in *The Philosophy of G. E. Moore*, ed. P. A. Schilpp (Evanston, Ill., 1942).

2. A less flamboyant and better balanced study of Moore's "defence" is contained in the essay "George Edward Moore," in my book *Knowledge and Certainty*.

2. In a recent volume of essays on Moore by various writers,[3] there is an essay by J. N. Findlay in which he declares that my early interpretation of Moore was a "monumental misinterpretation." [4] Findlay goes on to ask why *Moore* never did *repudiate* Malcolm's interpretation? Why did Moore *allow* Malcolm to persuade many people that his "linguistic" interpretation was correct? [5] This is one of those rare cases in which a philosopher's question gets answered: for in another essay in the same volume Morris Lazerowitz testifies that in a discussion in Cambridge, Moore told him that he *accepted* Malcolm's "linguistic" interpretation.[6] That would seem to be a satisfactory explanation of why Moore did not repudiate it!

3. Moore's response to skeptical arguments and views continued to puzzle and fascinate me. After brooding on the matter for some years, I published in 1949 an article impertinently entitled "Defending Common Sense" [7] in which I turned *against* Moore's "defence of common sense." I argued that Moore actually *misused* the expressions "know" and "know with certainty," when he made assertions such as "I know I am a human being," or "I know with certainty that that's a tree." Unwittingly, my article played a part in the genesis of Wittgenstein's final notebooks, which have been published under the title *Über Gewissheit— On Certainty*. Wittgenstein came to visit me in Ithaca just after my article had appeared. I made some mention of it, and Wittgenstein wanted me to read part of it to him, which I did. This precipitated a series of discussions between us, of which I gave a partial account in my Memoir of Wittgenstein.[8] I did not learn until several years later that Wittgenstein had kept on thinking and writing about the subject matter of those discussions. The final notebook entry occurred only two days

3. *G. E. Moore: Essays in Retrospect*, ed. A. Ambrose and M. Lazerowitz (New York, 1970).

4. J. N. Findlay, "Some Neglected Issues in the Philosophy of G. E. Moore," ibid., p. 66.

5. Ibid., p. 68.   6. Ibid., p. 109.

7. Malcolm, *Philosophical Review* 58 (1949).

8. Malcolm, *Ludwig Wittgenstein: A Memoir* (Oxford, 1958), pp. 87–93.

before his death. This is the origin of the most sustained study that Wittgenstein ever devoted to any aspect of Moore's thought.[9]

4. I had sent an offprint of my "Defending Common Sense" to Moore. In a letter of June 1949 he made a carefully stated reply. In my article I had tried to characterize the circumstances in which a remark such as "I know that that's a tree," or "It's perfectly certain that that's a tree," is properly made. I believe my characterization was inadequate but that my general point was valid, this point being that remarks of that kind cannot be made in just *any* situation but require *special* circumstances. I had imagined, in my article, that some people were seated in an open-air theater, the stage of which was bordered by trees. The stage scenery was painted to represent a woodland, and the painting was so skillfully executed that those people disagreed as to whether what they saw on one side of the stage was a real tree or instead a section of stage scenery. If they had approached nearer to the stage in order to decide this matter, it might have occurred as they came nearer that one of them would exclaim, "It's *certain* that that's a tree." This would

9. In the preface to the English translation of *On Certainty*, the editors report that Wittgenstein "had long been interested" in Moore's claim to *know* such propositions as "Here is a hand" and "The earth existed long before my birth" (*On Certainty*, trans. D. Paul and G. E. M. Anscombe [Oxford, 1969], p. vi). I am doubtful of the accuracy of that report. Wittgenstein had remarked to me in Cambridge in 1946–1947 that the only work of Moore's that greatly impressed him was Moore's discovery of what Wittgenstein labeled "Moore's paradox" (Wittgenstein, *Philosophical Investigations*, Part II, Sec. x). I asked, in protest, whether he didn't agree that Moore's "defence of common sense" was an important idea. Wittgenstein gave an affirmative nod of the head; but I had the definite impression that this part of Moore's thought had not much occupied him. I should add that Wittgenstein once said to me that Moore's lecture, "Proof of An External World," delivered to the British Academy, would have been a *ridiculous* performance had *anyone other than Moore* given it. I think he meant that Moore's integrity and deep seriousness, not the philosophical content of the "Proof," was what gave value to the lecture. My belief is that what transpired in Ithaca was not that a long-standing interest of Wittgenstein's was restimulated, but rather that he suddenly became absorbed in a subject matter that had not previously captured his attention.

have been a natural use of those words. In contrast, I argued, if there had been no disagreement or doubt about this matter, no question raised or inquiry started, then it would have been a misuse of language if one of those people had declared, "It's *certain* that that's a tree," or "I *know* it's a tree."

I should mention that Moore and I had sharply disagreed over this subject in our discussions of 1946–1947. When we sat in the back garden of his home on Chesterton Road, arguing over the concepts of knowledge and certainty, Moore, wanting to give an example of something he knew for certain, would point at a tree a few feet away, and say, with peculiar emphasis, "I *know* that *that's a tree.*" He would then claim that he had just made an assertion that was perfectly meaningful (as well as true); and I would dispute this claim.

5. I am going to quote a passage from Moore's letter to me in which he is referring to the imaginary person of my article who went closer to the stage to settle the question that had arisen, and who, when he had got closer, exclaimed, "It's *certain* that that's a tree." I quote Moore's remarks at length because they present a fundamental issue. Moore says the following of the man who went closer to the stage:

Whether his assertion is true or not depends solely on what is the case at the moment when he speaks, not at all on what has been the case just before, although it would not have been natural for him to use the expression unless, just before [he] had *not* . . . been in the condition in which [he is] now. It is something which has been brought about by the nearer approach, which makes his assertion true; and this, which has been brought about by the nearer approach, & which is rightly called . . . "knowing for certain that" the object in question "is a real tree," is identical with what was the case with me (& with you), when, sitting in my garden two years ago, I pointed or nodded at the young walnut-tree & said "I know that that is a tree." You wanted then, and want now, to say that my use of that expression was a "misuse" & "incorrect"; but the only reason you give for saying so is that I used it *under circumstances* under which it would not ordinarily be used, e.g., under the circumstances that there neither was at the moment nor *had been just previously* any doubt whether it was a tree or not. But that I used it *under circumstances* under which it would not ordinarily be used is no reason at all for saying I misused it or used it incorrectly, if, though this was so, I was using it *in the sense* in which it is ordinarily used—was using it to make the assertion which it is ordinarily used to make; and the argument I've just given is an argument designed to show that I was using it in the ordinary *sense*, though not under any ordinary circumstances. It would, it seems to me, be used in exactly the *sense* in which I was using it, by anyone who said, on a sufficiently near approach to the stage in your example, "Now I know for certain that it is a real tree;" the only difference being that in my case the use of the words was not preceded by a doubt, whereas in the other it was. If so, it follows that you were wrong not only in saying that mine was a misuse & incorrect, but also in saying that I was using the words in such a way that they "did not make sense." It seems to me you have been misled into saying this latter partly at least through having failed to notice an ambiguity in our use of "senseless." If a person, under circumstances in which everybody would see quite clearly that a certain object was a tree, were to keep repeatedly pointing at it & saying "That's a tree" or "I know that's a tree," we might well say that that was a senseless thing for him to do, & therefore, in a sense, a senseless thing for him to say; & even if he said it only once, under such circumstances, we might well say that it was a senseless thing for him to do—meaning, in all these cases, that it was a sort of thing which a sensible person wouldn't do, because, under those circumstances, it could serve no useful purpose to say those words. . . . But this is an entirely different thing from saying that the words in question don't, on that occasion "make sense," if by this is meant something which would follow from the proposition that they were not being used in their ordinary sense. It is perfectly possible that a person who uses them senselessly, in the sense that he uses them where no sensible person would use them because, under those circumstances, they serve no useful purpose, should be using them *in their normal sense*, & that what he asserts by so using them should be *true*. Of course, in my case, I was using them with a purpose—the purpose of disproving a general proposition which many philosophers have made; so that I was not only using them in their usual sense, but also under circumstances where they might possibly serve a useful purpose, though not a purpose for which they would commonly be used. It seems to me absurd that you should say that my usage was a "misuse" & "incorrect," merely because I used them under circumstances under which they would not commonly be used, when in fact I used them in exactly *the same sense* in which they are commonly used.

6.   These remarks of Moore's are lucid and strong. On first consideration they *seem* to be exactly right. They surely would be approved by those philosophers who believe that in regard to any indicative sentence S, it is important to distinguish between three different kinds of conditions, namely, first, conditions that determine whether S has *meaning* or *sense* ("meaning-conditions"), second, conditions that determine whether the proposition that S expresses (or that a speaker expresses in uttering S) is *true* or *false* ("truth-conditions"), and third, conditions that determine whether it is "appropriate" to utter, say, or assert S ("assertion-conditions"). Some philosophers might want to equate meaning-conditions with truth-conditions.[10] But for the appraisal of Moore's letter I think this issue may not be important. What does require attention is the supposed distinction between meaning-conditions and assertion-conditions. Failure to observe this distinction leads philosophers into serious error, it is claimed. For example, John Searle attributes Wittgenstein's seemingly paradoxical remarks about the sentence "I *know* I'm in pain" to what Searle calls "the assertion fallacy." This is the fallacy of confusing the conditions for the performance of the speech act of assertion with the analysis of the meaning of particular words occurring in certain assertions.[11]

7.   It is worth noting that Searle misreads Wittgenstein. Searle says, "Wittgenstein points out that under normal conditions, when I have a pain, it would be odd to say, 'I know I am in pain'." [12] Searle refers the reader to *Investigations*, para. 246. But in 246 Wittgenstein does not say that "under normal conditions" it would be "odd" to say "I know I'm in pain." He does make a remark about the familiar philosophical proposition that *only I can know* whether I'm in pain. He says that this is partly false, and partly nonsense. He clearly means that the false part is the assertion that

10. John Searle seems to favor this equation. He says, "The older philosophers were not wrong when they said: to know the meaning of a proposition is to know under what conditions it is true or false" (Searle, *Speech Acts* [London, 1969], p. 125).
11. Ibid., p. 141.   12. Ibid.

others cannot know whether I'm in pain, and that the part that is nonsense (*unsinning*) is the claim that I *know* whether I'm in pain. Wittgenstein adds this remark: "It can't be said of me at all (except perhaps as a joke) that I *know* I am in pain. What is it supposed to mean—except perhaps that I *am* in pain?" Now Searle thinks it is "odd" to say "I *know* I'm in pain." But here is where the distinction between meaning-conditions and assertion-conditions is supposed to be important. One condition governing assertions, according to Searle, is that one doesn't say what is *too obvious* to be worth saying; and, he says, "It's obviously true that when I have a pain, I know I have it." [13] We don't say what is obvious; that I know whether I'm in pain is obvious; therefore we don't say it. But, Searle implies, *if* we did say it we would *not* be misusing the word "know"!

A. J. Ayer expresses the same idea: "We find it silly for someone to tell us that he knows that he is in pain, because if he is in pain we take it for granted that he knows it." [14] I disagree with Ayer and Searle. Their contention that whenever I am in pain I *know* it, is, I believe, a misuse of the word "know." In my essay "The Privacy of Experience," [15] I undertook to demonstrate this by describing the various jobs that the expression "I know" normally does when it occurs as a prefix to a full sentence ("I know that *p*"), and then further showing that "I know" cannot do any of those normal jobs when it is prefixed to "I am in pain."

8. I do not, however, want to resume that particular battle here. The purpose of this digression from Moore was to point out the resemblance between what Moore thinks about the sentence "I know that's a tree" and what Ayer and Searle think about the sentence "I know I'm in pain." There can indeed be many reasons why it would be *inappropriate* to say a certain thing—because (for example) it would be misleading, irrelevant, distracting, rude, un-

13. Ibid., pp. 141–142.   14. A. J. Ayer, *The Concept of a Person,* p. 59.
15. Published in *Epistemology,* ed. A. Stroll (New York, 1967). Republished in the present volume, Essay 5.

fair, to mention a few possibilities. These reasons do not signify that *if* one did say the thing one would be making a *conceptual* error. Another reason why it might be inappropriate to say a particular thing is that saying it "would serve no useful purpose." This is the explanation that Moore offers of why (in the special circumstances to which Moore was referring) it would be, in a sense, "senseless" to say, "I *know* that's a tree." It would seem that Ayer and Searle have the same reason for declaring that it would be "odd" or "silly" for a person to say, "I *know* I'm in pain": saying this could serve no useful purpose because, they think, it is so *obvious* to everyone that someone who is in pain *knows* it. Moore, too, was appealing to the "obvious." According to him it was pointless for him to say to me (when we were sitting a few feet from a walnut-tree), "I know that's a tree": it was pointless because superfluous, Moore thought, since it was already *obvious to me* both that the thing to which Moore was referring was a tree and that Moore knew it was a tree. Therefore there was nothing conceptually but at most only something "conversationally" wrong with his assertion.

9. Moore's view is harder to criticize than is the Ayer-Searle position, partly for the reason that the words "I know I'm in pain" are never said, except humorously, in everyday language, whereas (in contrast) a number of Moore's examples of things he claims to know are expressed in sentences that commonly occur in ordinary discourse.

I want to undertake, in the present essay, a fresh assessment of Moore's "defence of common sense." What I believe now is that it contains several different layers of meaning; there is more going on there than I had previously recognized. My former interpretations of Moore have not been so much incorrect as incomplete.

Going back to Moore's letter, something that is striking and also perplexing in it is Moore's insistence that he was using the words "I *know* that's a tree" *in the ordinary sense* of those words, although *not in circumstances* in which they would ordinarily be used. One thing I want to ask is, How could Moore *tell* that he was using those words in "their ordinary sense"? Admittedly the circumstances were peculiar. Is the *sense* of the words something that can be *isolated* from the circumstances in which they are spoken? Suppose (what is not true) that "I know . . ." was said in daily language *only* to remove someone's doubt. *Could* those words have their ordinary sense if said in circumstances where neither the speaker nor anyone else could think that saying them would remove a doubt?

10.   Moore's remarks suggest to me a particular philosophical picture of sense or meaning, namely, that the sense of a sentence is, as it were, *attached* to the sentence and is present whenever the sentence is spoken (or perhaps, whenever it is spoken "deliberately"). It is the picture that Wittgenstein was referring to when he wrote, "We don't get free of the idea that the sense of a sentence accompanies the sentence: is there alongside of it." [16] I believe that Moore was deeply influenced by this idea, as are many philosophers. I think that the same idea was a powerful force in shaping Wittgentein's *Tractatus*. This idea is reflected in the conception of that book that in order to understand the sense of a sentence *all* one needs to know is the meaning of its elementary parts. At *Tractatus* 4.024 it is said of a sentence (any sentence): "One understands it, if one understands its constituents." [17] On this view, the sense of a sentence is solely a function of the meaning of its constituent words. Given the same words with the same meanings in the same order, the sentence will necessarily have the same sense. One aspect of Wittgenstein's later rejection of "the picture theory" of the *Tractatus* was his new conviction that *the circumstances* in which a sentence is used determine its sense. For example:

You say to me: "You understand this expression, don't you? Well then—I am using it in the sense you are familiar with,"—As if the sense were an atmosphere accompanying the word, which it carried with it into every kind of application.
    If, for example, someone says that the sentence "This is here" (saying

16. Wittgenstein, *Zettel*, para. 139.
17. Wittgenstein, *Tractatus Logico-Philosophicus* (London, 1922).

which he points to an object in front of him) makes sense to him, then he should ask himself in what special circumstances this sentence is actually used. There it does make sense.[18]

A philosopher says that he understands the sentence "I am here," that he means something by it, thinks something—even when he never considers how, on what occasions, this sentence is used.[19]

These remarks could have been appropriately addressed to Moore. In response to Moore's assertion, in his letter, that he was using the sentence "I *know* that's a tree" in its ordinary sense, although not in ordinary circumstances, I want to protest: "How can that be? What conception do you have of 'the sense' of a sentence, if you think that the circumstances in which the sentence is spoken have nothing to do with its sense?"

11.   Another thing in Moore's letter that perplexes me is his insistence that he was using the words "I *know* that's a tree" in "their ordinary sense," as if he thought there was one and only one sense in which those words are used in everyday language. I confess that I do not have any exact feeling for alleged different "senses" of a sentence. But it is easy to illustrate different ways in which a sentence is *used*. I conceive of these different uses of a sentence as functions of the different circumstances in which the sentence is spoken or written. If someone wants to maintain, as did Moore, that when a sentence is employed in a number of different ways it nevertheless has *the same sense*, then I think that this contention is too nebulous to be capable of either proof or refutation; yet at the same time it can be shown to be a misleading philosophical image.

12.   I shall now undertake to describe some of the ways in which a sentence of the form "I know that so-and-so" is used in actual language. I do not propose to offer a complete account; indeed, I think there is no such thing as a "complete" account. I realize that the following details may be boring, but I hope that an illuminating

18. Wittgenstein, *Investigations*, para. 117.   19. Ibid., para. 514.

overview of the varied uses of the expression "I know" will emerge.

In his attempted rebuttals of skepticism Moore habitually speaks in the first-person, singular, present tense: "I *know* that this is a hand, that I am a human being, that the earth existed long before I was born," and so on. Because of this, I too will confine myself to describing different employments of the words "I know" in their occurrence as a prefix to propositional expressions. It may be thought that this is already an error, for the reason that "I know that *p*" (said by speaker S) is true if and only if "He knows that *p*" (said about speaker S) is true, and that therefore, by concentrating on the first person use of "know," I will be *mistaking* the circumstances in which it is or is not socially or conversationally "appropriate" to say "I know . . . ," for features of *the concept* of knowing something. I disagree. From the fact that there is a "truth equivalence," in the foregoing sense, between "I know . . ." and "He knows . . . ," it does not follow that the differences in their use are irrelevant to the concept of knowing something. This is easily shown by the example of "I'm in pain" (said by S) and "He's in pain" (said about S). These two have the same truth-value, yet the second is properly employed on the basis of observations of behavior, whereas the other one is not. And *this* difference is surely a feature of *the concept* of pain.

13.   Let us consider, then, the following cases:

1) There is a committee meeting at which Mr. N was supposed to be present, but so far he has not arrived. One person says, "Perhaps he forgot." Another replies, "I know he didn't forget, because he told me only ten minutes ago that he would be here."

In this example the expression "I know that not-*p*" was used to introduce the presentation of evidence that not-*p*, evidence that the speaker already had in his possession. Here, "I know that not-*p*" is like saying, "I have the following evidence that not-*p*, namely. . . ."

2) Someone has done a computation that is needed in a certain

activity. He says: "Here is the result. I know it's right; I checked it three times."

In this case, "I know it's right" was not used to introduce the proof (i.e., the actual computation): instead it amounted to the claim that an adequate checking procedure had been carried out. "I know it's right" came to the same here as "I checked it." It was implied that further checking was needless.

3) A and B are discussing a chess game that Mr. N just lost. A says: "Perhaps N would have won if he had moved his bishop like *this.*" B replies: "No. I know he couldn't have won with that move." A says: "Why not?" B says: "Well, let's consider it," and then proceeds to work out a proof that this move could not have saved N.

Unlike case 1), the proof was not yet in B's possession when he said, "I know that not-*p*." Here, "I know that not-*p*" came to the same as "I can prove that not-*p*."

4) A casual conversation between strangers: "I hear it's been discovered that aspirin is poisonous." "I know that's not true." "How do you know?" "That's my line of work—I'm a biochemist."

In this case, "I know" was used to claim competence in a general area, rather than to claim particular evidence about aspirin. This scientist probably had never investigated aspirin; but if this alleged discovery had been made he would undoubtedly have known about it.

5) Two strangers are talking about an opera singer. One says: "With her fame, beauty, and wealth, she must live a marvelous life." The other replies: "You're wrong. I know that actually she is lonely and unhappy." "How do you know?" "I'm her manager" (sister, closest friend).

5) is similar to 4), and yet is different in that the speaker does not assert his expertise in some general domain of knowledge, but instead claims a close personal relationship with the singer.

6) It is said that professional "chicken sexers" can accurately distinguish the sex of newly born chicks, without being able to point

out any differences in physical characteristics. In response to the question "Are you sure *this* chick is male?" a trained chicken sexer would be entitled to reply, "I *know* it's male," without being able to give any proof or evidence. In the U.S. Navy there is (or was) training in aircraft recognition, which involves looking at photographs of aircraft, projected on a screen with increasingly reduced viewing time. This training produces the ability to identify aircraft accurately, with a viewing time of 1/125 of a second or less. At this speed one does not pick out distinguishing characteristics. A person with this training would be entitled to say, "I know that was a JU-88," without being able to give any evidence. There are many pedestrian examples of similar abilities, such as being able to pick out one's raincoat from similar coats in a cloak room, without being able to specify any distinguishing marks; or being able to note that there has been some rearrangement of the furniture in a familiar room, without being able to specify what the change is.

It would be wrong to say that in these cases there is only "subjective certainty" and not knowledge. The fact that there is an ability to repeatedly make correct judgments justifies the use of "I know."

7) Two people at a horse race: "Smiler will win this one." "What makes you think so?" "I have a very strong hunch. I *know* he'll win. I'm going to bet on him."

Here there is no authority, evidence, or (I am assuming) ability to pick winners. In this case, "I know" is used just like "I'm certain." It expresses mere "subjective certainty." It is worth noting that it would be permissible to say, "You were right," if Smiler won, and "You were wrong," if Smiler lost, regardless of whether the confident one had said "I'm certain" or "I know."

8) A mother is anxious that her daughter should practise for her piano lesson. When instead the girl settles down before the television, the mother says: "You have a piano lesson tomorrow." The irritated daughter replies: "I *know* I have a lesson tomorrow."

In this use of "I know," there is no implication of evidence, authority, ability, or even certainty (either subjective or objective). In this case, "I *know* that *p*" is employed like "I don't need to be reminded that *p*." (I owe this example to Elizabeth Wolgast).

9) A friend is frightened of the surgery he is about to undergo. You are not a doctor and have no information about this operation. But you say to him: "Don't be anxious. I *know* you're going to be *all right.*"

What your "I know" does here is to provide comfort, encouragement, support.

10) Two people are working late on a problem. One says: "We're too tired to do any more work tonight." The other says: "I know it. Let's stop."

Here, "I know that *p*" is used like "I agree that *p*." There is no question of evidence, proof, authority, or ability. One is expressing agreement. (I owe this sort of example to David Reeve).

11) A friend's eyesight has begun to fail. One day you ask him, "How is your vision?" He replies: "It's getting pretty bad. But I know *that's* a *tree*"—pointing at a tree a few feet away.

In this case, "I know *that's* a *tree*" is used like "My sight is still good enough to make out that tree."

12) I lead a blind man into a room and wish to seat him in a chair. Once previously I seated him on a stool, from which he subsequently fell and hurt himself. This time, when I say "Here's a chair," he asks anxiously, "Are you *sure* it's a *chair?*" I reply: "Yes. I *know* it's a *chair.*"

With these words I am reassuring the blind man, urging him to trust me, encouraging him to *do* something—to sit down. In this example, "I know that *p*" comes to much the same as "You can rely on me that *p*."

It is especially interesting to compare this example with the situation of Moore's saying to another philosopher in a philosophical discussion, "I *know* that that's a chair." Moore would not be reassuring the other one that it's a chair, or meaning "You can rely on me," or encouraging the other one to sit in that chair. Nor could the other philosopher "verify for himself" that it is a chair—whereas the blind man could do this by touch.

14. Let us see what illumination can be gained from this survey of a dozen examples of different circumstances in which sentences of the form "I know that *p*" may be used. It is evident that in those different situations the speakers would be *doing* different things and *saying* different things. My particular concern is with the locution "I know." My aim is to show that this locution does *different jobs*, achieves different things, in different circumstances. We could put it like this: Sometimes "I know . . ." can be paraphrased as "I have the following evidence . . ." sometimes as "I have checked it"; sometimes as "I can prove it"; sometimes as "I am certain . . ."; sometimes as "I agree . . ."; sometimes as "You can rely on me . . ."; and so on.

At this point some philosophers will want to exclaim: "You can speak of different 'paraphrases' if you like. But these different paraphrases merely reflect different 'conversational implications.' The sense, the meaning, of 'I know . . .' remains *the same* throughout those different situations you described. Moore was *right* in declaring that he used the words 'I know that's a tree' in *their ordinary sense.*"

I confess to finding this objection baffling. *I* have no perception of a constant, one and the same, sense. But of course this is a clumsy way for me to express myself—as if I knew what to look for but could not find it. What I do perceive is that in one of the cases I described, the speaker who said "I know . . ." was, in and by saying that, *agreeing with* the other person; in another case he was not agreeing with but instead *reassuring* the other; in still another case he was doing neither of these things but instead *informing* the other that he has *convincing evidence* on the matter; and so on. All of this lies on the surface, clearly revealed in the differing circumstances of the cases. There is nothing here for speculation. The view I want to reject appars to hold that these observable differences in the jobs that "I know . . ." does in the various cases do not disclose the *essential meaning* of "I know . . . ," which is there behind the differing circumstances.

My response to this conception is to say that I do not understand what the "essential meaning" of "I know . . ." is, and that I do not see the necessity for believing in such a thing. How does one recognize it? How is it related to those different jobs that the locution "I know . . ." does in actual cases?

The bafflement that the objection creates is the same that I felt when, sitting with Moore in his garden, he would point at the nearby tree and declare, with emphasis, "I *know* that *that's* a tree!" I felt a mental paralysis; I could not get hold of the meaning of Moore's sentence. I had told Wittgenstein of those discussions and the following remarks from his notebooks show that he had a similar reaction:

"I know that that's a tree." Why does it strike me as if I did not understand the sentence? though it is after all an extremely simple sentence of the most ordinary kind? It is as if I could not focus my mind on any meaning. Because I do not search for the focus in that province where the meaning is. As soon as I think of an everyday employment of the sentence instead of a philosophical one, its meaning becomes clear and ordinary.[20]

15. It is evident that Moore was not giving *any* everyday employment to the words "I know. . . ." Nor was he using them in "*the* ordinary sense"—there seems to be no such thing. But I certainly do not conclude that Moore was talking nonsense. He was giving a *philosophical* employment to the words "I know. . . ." He was saying something of deep philosophical interest. Now he could have been expressing a philosophical insight, or a philosophical error. I believe he did both. I think that his philosophical assertions of the form "I know . . ." have a highly complex meaning—they contain several layers, or veins, of meaning: which is to say that there are several different, correct, interpretations of his philosophical message.

16. First, there is the "linguistic" interpretation. This was not a "monumental misinterpretation," but a true, and yet incomplete,

20. Wittgenstein, *On Certainty*, para. 347. Here and elsewhere I depart slightly from the Paul-Anscombe translation.

interpretation. Moore was outraged by the contentions of the skeptical philosophers. He saw very clearly that those contentions do
violence to ordinary language. Here is a typical expression of his
feeling in this matter, presented in a public lecture:

Suppose, that now, instead of saying, "I am inside a building," I were to
say "I think I'm inside a building, but perhaps I'm not: it's not *certain* that
I am," or instead of saying "I have got some clothes on," I were to say "I
think I've got some clothes on, but it's just possible that I haven't." Would
it not sound rather ridiculous for me now, under these circumstances, to
say "I *think* I've got some clothes on" or even to say "I not only think I
have, I know that it is very likely indeed that I have, but I can't be quite
sure?" [21]

Moore's satirical thrusts against skepticism struck me and others
like a thunderbolt! Awaking as from a dream, we realized that it
would indeed have been ridiculous for Moore to have said to his
audience, "I believe I have some clothes on, but it's possible I
haven't." This was a revelation for which many are grateful to
Moore.

17. But, this insight led Moore into an error. (This is the second
layer of meaning.) His perception of the absurdity of saying, in
that situation, "I don't know if I have clothes on," drew him into
the assumption that it would be correct to say "I *know* I have
clothes on." Yet what Moore had actually perceived was that nothing in that situation made a doubt as to whether he had clothes on
intelligible. He should have concluded that *both* "I don't know" and
"I know" were out of place in that context. "I know" is often used
to express the *absence* of doubt. But the *absence of doubt* and the *unin-
telligibility of doubt* are very different things. Wittgenstein says in
the *Investigations*, " 'I know . . . may mean 'I do not doubt . . .
but does not mean that the words 'I doubt . . . are *senseless*, that
doubt is logically excluded." [22] Wittgenstein is referring here to the
way that "I know . . ." is used in ordinary language. He is saying,

21. Moore, *Philosophical Papers* (New York, 1959), pp. 227–228.
22. Wittgenstein, *Investigations*, p. 221.

correctly, that this expression is not used *in ordinary language* to make a *conceptual, philosophical* point. But this is the kind of point that Moore needed to make, namely, the point that the statement "It is uncertain that I have clothes on" would be a conceptual absurdity in that situation. I suspect that Moore was misled here by the assumption of Excluded Middle: "Either I know it or I don't know it." He perceived that "I don't know it" *couldn't* be said, and wrongly concluded that "I know it" must therefore be right and true. I will call this the "Excluded Middle" interpretation.

18.   I come now to the third vein of meaning, which could be termed an "introspective" interpretation. Recall how Moore claimed that, when in philosophical discussion he said "I know that that's a tree," he was using those words in "the ordinary sense." I said against this that it does not appear that there is such a thing as *"the* ordinary sense" of those words. The question that now interests me is: What did Moore imagine to be "the ordinary sense" of those words?

Remember that in his letter to me he declared that when someone says "I know that that's a tree," whether the speaker's assertion is true or not "depends solely on what is the case at the moment he speaks." Moore also said that whether the assertion is true depends on "the condition" in which the speaker is: when the assertion is true this condition "is rightly called 'knowing that' the object in question is a tree." Thus it appears that, according to Moore, when a speaker is employing the words "I know that that's a tree" in "their ordinary sense," he is stating that he is in the condition (state) of knowing that the object referred to is a tree.

This way of specifying "the ordinary sense" of the words may not seem helpful. It looks tautological. I believe, however, that it provides a clue. It presents a picture of how Moore conceived the matter.

In order to make the picture more explicit we need to ask, What *kind* of "state" did Moore conceive knowing to be? I will put forward the suggestion that Moore was tempted by the notion that the state of *knowing* that the thing at which he pointed was a tree had the same sort of "immediacy" and "indubitability" as do states of sensation, feeling, or mood. Many philosophers have wanted to say of such states as feeling drowsy or ill, or embarrassed or bored or cheerful, that they are states of which one can be, perhaps *must* be, "directly aware." My suggestion is that Moore thought of *knowing* or *knowing with certainty* in the same way.

Is it plausible to attribute such an idea to Moore? Let us notice, first, that this idea exists as a definite temptation in philosophy. To illustrate this, I quote from Moore's contemporary, Prichard: "We must recognize that whenever we know something we either do, or at least can, by reflecting, directly know that we are knowing it, and that whenever we believe something, we similarly either do or can directly know that we are believing it and not knowing it." [23] Prichard characterizes a person's knowing something as a "condition" or "state" of that person, just as Moore does. I quote again from Prichard: "We must recognize that when we know something we either do, or by reflecting can, know that our condition is one of knowing that thing, while when we believe something, we either do or can know that our condition is one of believing and not of knowing: so that we cannot mistake belief for knowledge or vice versa." [24] In declaring that we do or can "directly know" whether we know something or merely believe it, Prichard seems to be holding that both knowledge and belief are states of oneself that one can infallibly identify and distinguish by reflection or introspective observation.

No one realizes better than I do that Moore was not Prichard. Yet it may help our understanding of Moore if we take note of this temptation to conceive of a person's knowing something as a state of which that person can have "direct knowledge" or "immediate awareness." The implication of this conception would be that a person can determine by reflection whether he knows a certain

23. H. A. Prichard, *Knowledge and Perception* (Oxford, 1950), p. 86.
24. Ibid., p. 88.

thing or merely believes it, and *without any possibility of being mistaken!*

Now when someone says such a thing as "I feel ill" or "I feel embarrassed," understands the language, and is being truthful, his utterance has the following three logical features: first, it is not subject to *error;* second, it is neither supported by nor supportable by *evidence;* third, it cannot be confirmed or disconfirmed by any *investigation.* My suggestion is that when Moore, in criticizing skepticism, produced his illustrations of things he *knew,* he was endowing his claims to know those things with these same three logical features. First of all, he regarded the possibility of his being *wrong* as simply having no application to those claims. When he said to his British Academy audience, "Here is one hand, and here is another," and further asserted that this was something he *knew,* he added the following remarks: "How absurd it would be to suggest that I did not know it, but only believed it, and that perhaps it was not the case! You might as well suggest that I do not know that I am now standing up and talking—that perhaps after all I'm not, and that it's not quite certain that I am!" [25] Moore seemed to be declaring that to speak of *the possibility of his being wrong* simply made no sense. Secondly, in *the philosophical situation* where Moore refers to some object and asserts that he *knows* that it's a tree or a hand, since his philosophical auditors are just as good at identifying trees or hands as Moore is, and since they have just as good view of the object as Moore does, there is nothing that Moore can do in the way of presenting *evidence* for his claims. The peculiarity of the circumstances in which he makes his claims eliminates the applicability of "evidence." Thirdly, because of these same circumstances it would be senseless to propose a closer look, or any other *investigation,* to determine whether the object to which Moore refers really is what he says it is.

It is a striking fact that Moore's attempts to give examples of things he "knows" or "knows with certainty" have the result that

25. Moore, *Philosophical Papers*, pp. 146–147.

his claims take on several of the major logical features of first-person declarations of feeling or mood. Moore, unlike Prichard, would never have put forward *the thesis* that knowledge is always a self-revealing mental state. But when in philosophical lectures or discussions he tried to give *examples* of his own knowledge, the concepts of evidence, investigation, and possibility of error seemed to be deprived of the application they normally have to claims to know something. Moore's knowledge-claims apparently display a surprising amount of the logic of first-person declarations of sensation, feeling, or mood.

In thinking about this matter I reread my account of a conversation that Wittgenstein and I had in Ithaca, in which he made this observation:

> Moore would like to stare at a house that is only 20 feet away and say, with a peculiar intonation, "I *know there's* a *house!*" He does this because he wants to produce in himself the *feeling* of knowing. He wants to exhibit *knowing for certain* to himself. In this way he has the idea that he is replying to the skeptical philosopher who claims that everyday examples of knowing that there is a dog in the backyard, or that the neighbour's house is on fire, are not really or strictly *knowledge*, are not knowledge *in the highest degree.* It is as if someone had said "You don't really feel pain when you are pinched" and Moore then pinched himself in order to feel the pain, and thus to prove to himself that the other is wrong. Moore treats the sentence "I know so & so" like the sentence "I have a pain." [26]

Subsequently Wittgenstein wrote in a notebook the following remark: "The wrong use made by Moore of the proposition 'I know . . .' lies in his regarding it as an utterance as little subject to doubt as 'I am in pain.' And since from 'I know it is so' there follows 'It is so,' then the latter can't be doubted either." [27]

This "introspective" interpretation of Moore's "defence of common sense" gains plausibility, I believe, when one considers the peculiar way in which the controversy goes on between Moore and his skeptical opponents. The latter may declare themselves in the following manner:

26. Malcolm, *Wittgenstein: A Memoir*, pp. 87–88.
27. Wittgenstein, *On Certainty*, para. 178.

You *believe* that you are a human being, that you live on the earth, that it existed many years before you were born, that you are wearing clothes and standing before some people, that there are windows in that wall and a door in this one. You are *convinced* of all those things. And they *may* all be true; probably they are true. But you do not *know* they are; you do not know this with certainty.

Now note the odd way in which Moore confronted that skepticism in "A Defence of Common Sense." He spoke as follows: "Don't I really *know* those things? Is it possible that I merely believe them? In answer to this question, I think I have nothing better to say than that it seems to me that I *do* know them with certainty." [28] In real life if one person declares, "I know that so-and-so," and another retorts, "You may *believe* it, but you don't *know* it," you would expect them to go on to consider the nature and quality of *the evidence* that so-and-so. In the controversy between Moore and the skeptics this does not occur. What evidence *could* Moore offer to his philosophical opponents to convince them that he is a human being or that he is holding up his hand? When Moore responds to the skeptic his attention is not focused outwardly on evidence, but inwardly on his own mental state. He *seems* to take the skeptic about knowledge to be challenging Moore's declaration as to what Moore's own mental state is. And Moore feels called upon to respond with a careful, introspective discrimination. It looks as if Moore asks himself, "Is my present state one of *knowing* that this is a hand, or is it instead the state of merely *believing* it? After reflection he declares: "It *seems* to me that my state is one of *knowing* it." Moore gives the impression of assuming that this dispute with the skeptic as to whether Moore *knows* that this thing is a hand can be resolved only by Moore *himself* (if it can be resolved at all) and only by his looking into his own mind. It is as if Moore thought as follows: "It is not easy to distinguish between the states of knowing and of believing. Nevertheless, when I pay attention to my present state it does definitely appear to me to be a state of knowing and not one of just believing."

28. Moore, *Philosophical Papers*, p. 44.

Let us return to Moore's problematic claim that he was using the words "I know that that's a tree" in "the ordinary sense," although not in "the ordinary circumstances." This claim is less obscure if viewed in the light of the hypothesis that Moore had some tendency to imagine that "the ordinary sense" of this sentence is that the speaker is in a particular mental state. This hypothesis, if correct, would help to explain why Moore believed that the utterance "I know that that's a tree" always has sense and the same sense, even in situations in which it would not "serve a useful purpose." The sense of the utterance would be this—that the speaker has (or is in) a certain mental state. The speaker would be disclosing what it is like in his mind!

This conception of the sense of "I know . . ." seems to me to be, in Wittgenstein's phrase, "a dream of our language." [29] I believe that we will see this if we reflect back on our dozen examples of the use of "I know. . . ." These examples indicate the *variety of work* that the prefix "I know . . ." does in actual language. It is used to claim the possession of evidence, or expertise, or ability; it is used to comfort, reassure, express agreement; it is used to say that one has thoroughly checked something, or that one can be relied on, or that one doesn't need to be reminded. And so on.

In one case, if I want to know whether *you know* that your calculation is correct, what I want to know is whether you *checked* it, not what your present mental state is. In another case, if I want to know whether *you know* that Jones will be married next week, what I want to know is whether you *heard the announcement* this morning, not what your mental state is this afternoon. In still another case, if I want to know whether *you know* that the hinges should be placed on the door this way rather than that way, it will satisfy me to learn that you are *a professional carpenter;* I am not seeking to learn about your present state of mind. These remarks of mine are not meant to deny that there can be a case where my interest in whether *you know* such and such is at least partly an inter-

29. Wittgenstein, *Investigations*, para. 358.

est in whether *your present feeling* on the matter is one of absolute conviction. This would genuinely be an interest in your present mental state; and what you yourself indicated to me about your degree of conviction would be of the utmost importance. But this would be only one kind of case. Our interest in whether someone knows this or that covers many kinds of cases in which there is no interest at all in feelings of conviction or certainty. To the extent that Prichard, and perhaps Moore too, had the idea that one could determine by reflection on one's own mental state whether one knows something or merely believes it, they were misrepresenting the greater part of the range of the concept of knowledge.

19.   I turn finally to the richest vein of meaning in Moore's attempt to give examples of things he knows, a vein mined by Wittgenstein in *On Certainty*. Wittgenstein's perception was that in the class of empirical propositions there are some propositions that are "unshakeable," that "stand fast," that are "exempt from doubt"; or, to state this point somewhat differently, those propositions are such that *if* they did come into doubt one's capacity to make *any* judgments would be destroyed. As Wittgenstein puts it, "about certain empirical propositions no doubt can exist if making judgments is to be possible at all." [30] Or again: "the *questions* that we raise and our *doubts* depend on the fact that some propositions are exempt from doubt, are as it were like hinges on which those turn." [31] This does not just mean that in any investigation there will be something that is not investigated, but rather that there are certain things that will not be investigated in any investigation, since the attempt to doubt and to investigate *those* things would throw into disarray one's understanding of what it is to investigate and to find out anything:

One cannot make experiments if there are not many things one does not doubt. But that does not mean that one takes certain presuppositions on good faith. When I write a letter and post it, I assume that it will arrive—

30. Wittgenstein, *On Certainty*, para. 308.   31. Ibid., para. 341.

I expect this. If I make an experiment I do not doubt the existence of the apparatus that is in front of my eyes. I have plenty of doubts, but not *that* one. If I do a calculation I believe, without any doubt, that the figures on the paper aren't switching of their own accord, and I also trust my memory the whole time, and trust it absolutely. The certainty here is the same as that of my never having been on the moon.[32]

Here Wittgenstein is deliberately drawing an analogy between those mentioned doubts that we *don't* have and Moore's "certainties," such as "I have never been far from the surface of the earth," "I am a human being," "This is my hand." Wittgenstein is extracting from Moore's "defence of common sense" an extremely important observation, namely, that "the framework" within which one's thinking occurs is constituted in part by propositions that are contingent and, in a sense, empirical: "I want to say: propositions of the form of empirical propositions and not only propositions of logic, belong to the foundation of all operating with thoughts (with language).—This observation is not of the form "I know . . . .". "I know . . ." states that *I* know, and that is not of logical interest."[33] Some philosophers would hold that one could doubt any particular contingent proposition without undermining one's ability to think. But is this true? Referring to the proposition "My name is L. W.," Wittgenstein says:

When I ask "Do I know or do I only believe that I am called . . ?", it is useless to look within myself.

But I could say: Not only do I never have the slightest doubt that I am called that, but there is no judgment I could be certain of if I started to doubt that.[34]

If my name is *not* L. W., how can I rely on what is meant by "true" and "false"?[35]

Wittgenstein tries to weigh the difference between the proposition "The water in the kettle on the gas-flame will not freeze but boil" and the proposition "The person opposite me is my old friend N. N.":

32. Ibid., para. 337.   33. Ibid., para. 401.   34. Ibid., para. 490.
35. Ibid., para. 515.

If I now say "I know that the water in the kettle on the gas-flame will not freeze but boil," I seem to be as justified in this "I know" as I am in *any*. 'If I know anything I know *this*.'—Or do I know with still *greater* certainty that the person opposite me is my old friend so-and-so? And how does that compare with the proposition that I am seeing with two *eyes* and shall see them if I look in the mirror?—I don't know with confidence what I should answer here.—But still there is a difference between the cases. If the water on the flame freezes, I shall of course be astonished in the highest degree, but I shall assume some factor I don't know of, and perhaps leave the matter to physicists to judge. But what could make me doubt whether this person here is N. N., whom I have known for years? Here a doubt would seem to drag everything with it and plunge it into chaos.[36]

Wittgenstein is suggesting that for each of us there are some propositions (different ones for you than for me) that are contingent and quasi-empirical, and yet have the following two features: First, they are "beyond doubt" in the sense that if one doubted them one would not be sure of anything, including one's understanding of one's own language ("If this deceives me, what does 'deceive' mean anymore?"),[37] and consequently one's ability to reason, to judge, to investigate, and *even to doubt*, would be crippled—to put it paradoxically, some doubts would make doubting impossible! Second, there would be nothing *unreasonable* in one's refusing to doubt these "framework" propositions, even in the face of the most astonishing happenings. As Wittgenstein puts it: "The question is this: What if you had to change your opinion even in these most fundamental things? And to that the answer appears to me to be: 'You don't *have* to change it. This is just what being "fundamental" is.' "[38] One part of Wittgenstein's perception is that we can engage in the activities of calculating, verifying, reasoning, questioning, only if we accept many things without question. We are taught the names of objects, and we are taught how to add and multiply. We accept what we are taught. To doubt at this level would mean that we were *not learning* to calculate, or to look for and fetch objects, or to carry out orders: "Something must be taught us as a foundation."[39] A foun-

36. Ibid., para. 613.   37. Ibid., para. 507.   38. Ibid., para. 512.
39. Ibid., para. 449.

dation must underlie every use of language: "Every language-game is based on words and objects being recognized again. We learn with the same inexorability that this is a chair as that $2 \times 2 = 4$." [40] Doubting at this level would have to involve an uncertainty about the meaning of the language in which the doubting is stated: "If, therefore, I doubt or am uncertain about this being my hand (in whatever sense), why not also about the meaning of these words?" [41] An implication I see in this remark is that a philosopher cannot express a genuine doubt by the sentence "I am in doubt whether this is a hand," since he should also doubt whether the word "hand" is the right name for that whose presence he wants to doubt. If we imagine this doubt being expressed in actions rather than words (e.g., in *uncertain* responses to commands such as "Hold out your hand"), then we picture a child who has not yet learned the word, or a retarded or senile adult. This brings out a respect in which a philosophical doubt that this is a hand is gainsaid by the very words it uses; and if it substituted *actions* for words it would be senility, not philosophy.

Another part of Wittgenstein's perception is that although Moore's declarations of the form "I know . . ." were actually misstatements, yet they also partly conceal and partly reveal a grand insight. Moore's declarations were wrong because, for one thing, of their *autobiographical* aspect: it is not a matter of philosophical import whether *Moore* knows this or that. Moore's statements were also wrong for the deeper reason that the expression "I know . . . ," like "I am in doubt . . . ," works within a framework where there can be reasons for doubt, further investigation, convincing evidence. "I know . . ." can also be used, as we saw, to express agreement, or to reassure, or to assert the speaker's competence, and so on. But Moore was not employing "I know . . ." in *any* of these ways, or in any ordinary way at all. Moore was responding to the metaphysical thesis that one *cannot* know this or that sort of thing. He was right in rejecting this thesis, but the way

40. Ibid., para. 455.   41. Ibid., para. 456.

he did it was wrong: "Moore's mistake lies in this—countering the assertion that one cannot know that, by saying 'I do know it.' " [42] Moore was trying to combat a metaphysical assertion with a metaphysical assertion of his own of the form "I know. . . ." Yet, as Wittgenstein remarks, "It is as if 'I know' did not tolerate a metaphysical emphasis." [43]

But although Moore expressed himself badly, using "I know . . ." in a confused way, we can rightly say, I believe, that Moore was catching hold of something of fundamental importance. It was a point that Moore himself could not articulate; this task was left for Wittgenstein: "When Moore says he *knows* such and such, he is really enumerating a lot of empirical propositions which we affirm without special testing; propositions, therefore, which have a peculiar logical role in the system of our empirical propositions." [44] Most of the propositions that Moore enumerates are undoubtedly contingent propositions, and in addition they seem to be empirical propositions. Yet they are not propositions which we think of questioning or testing. They are not propositions that are "known" or "not known." Their peculiar role is to define in part the boundaries within which we raise questions, make investigations, conjecture, verify, reason. Without such boundaries we would be speechless and thoughtless.

I think it is fair to say that Moore had no clear perception of this; nonetheless his achievement was impressive. In his time philosophical skepticism about perception, knowledge, the material world, was plausible and popular. It was the received doctrine (and currently it is being revived). I see Moore as a largely solitary figure, astonished by the claims of skepticism, not clearly understanding what his response should be, yet fully realizing the huge importance for philosophy of the issue, and therefore throwing down the gauntlet and standing fast! That was, to my mind, an outstanding example for the intellectual world, of courage and strength of character.

42. Ibid., para. 521.   43. Ibid., para. 482.   44. Ibid., para. 136.

Philosophy is more than doubly fortunate that Wittgenstein's previously only mild interest in Moore's "defence of common sense" suddenly became intensified, resulting in a brilliant new study of the logical boundaries of doubt, belief, and knowledge, and thereby revealing a dimension of depth in Moore's thought that would otherwise have gone unperceived.

9 | The Groundlessness of Belief

I

In his final notebooks Wittgenstein wrote that it is difficult "to realize the groundlessness of our believing." [1] He was thinking of how much mere acceptance, on the basis of no evidence, shapes our lives. This is obvious in the case of small children. They are told the names of things. They accept what they are told. They do not ask for grounds. A child does not demand a proof that the person who feeds him is called "Mama." Or are we to suppose that the child reasons to himself as follows: "The others present seem to know this person who is feeding me, and since they call her 'Mama' that probably is her name"? It is obvious on reflection that a child cannot consider evidence or even doubt anything until he has already learned much. As Wittgenstein puts it: "The child learns by believing the adult. Doubt comes *after* belief" (*OC*, 160).

What is more difficult to perceive is that the lives of educated, sophisticated adults are also formed by groundless beliefs. I do not mean eccentric beliefs that are out on the fringes of their lives, but

1. Ludwig Wittgenstein, *On Certainty*, ed. G. E. M. Anscombe and G. H. von Wright; trans. D. Paul and G. E. M. Anscombe (Oxford, 1969), paragraph 166. Henceforth I include references to this work in the text, employing the abbreviation "*OC*" followed by paragraph number. References to Wittgenstein's *The Blue and Brown Books* (Oxford, 1958) are indicated in the text by "*BB*" followed by page number. References to his *Philosophical Investigations*, ed. G. E. M. Anscombe and R. Rhees; trans. G. E. M. Anscombe (Oxford, 1967) are indicated by "*PI*" followed by paragraph number. In *OC* and *PI* I have mainly used the translations of Paul and Anscombe but with some departures.

fundamental beliefs. Take the belief that familiar material things (watches, shoes, chairs) do not cease to exist without some physical explanation. They don't "vanish in thin air." It is interesting that we do use that very expression: "I *know* I put the keys right here on this table. They must have vanished in thin air!" But this exclamation is hyperbole: we are not speaking in literal seriousness. I do not know of any adult who would consider, in all gravity, that the keys might have inexplicably ceased to exist.

Yet it is possible to imagine a society in which it was accepted that sometimes material things do go out of existence without having been crushed, melted, eroded, broken into pieces, burned up, eaten, or destroyed in some other way. The difference between those people and ourselves would not consist in their *saying* something that we don't say ("It vanished in thin air"), since we say it too. I conceive of those people as acting and thinking differently from ourselves in such ways as the following: if one of them could not find his wallet, he would give up the search sooner than you or I would; also he would be less inclined to suppose that it was stolen. In general what we would regard as convincing circumstantial evidence of theft those people would find less convincing. They would take fewer precautions than we would to protect their possessions against loss or theft. They would have less inclination to save money, since it too can just disappear. They would not tend to form strong attachments to material things. They would stand in a looser relation to the world than we do. The disappearance of a desired object, which would provoke us to a frantic search, they would be more inclined to accept with a shrug. Of course their scientific theories would be different; but also their attitude toward experiment, and inference from experimental results, would be more tentative. If the repetition of a familiar chemical experiment did not yield the expected result, this *could* be because one of the chemical substances had vanished.

The outlook I have sketched might be thought to be radically incoherent. I do not see that this is so. Although those people consider it to be possible that a wallet might have inexplicably ceased to exist, it is also true that they regard that as unlikely. For things that are lost usually do turn up later; or if not, their fate can often be accounted for. Those people use pretty much the same criteria of identity that we do; their reasoning would resemble ours quite a lot. Their thinking would not be incoherent. But it would be different, since they would leave room for possibilities that we exclude.

If we compare their view that material things do sometimes go out of existence inexplicably with our own rejection of that view, it does not appear to me that one position is supported by *better evidence* than is the other. Each position is compatible with ordinary experience. On the one hand it is true that familiar objects (watches, wallets, lawn-chairs) occasionally disappear without any adequate explanation. On the other hand it happens, perhaps more frequently, that a satisfying explanation of the disappearance is discovered.

Our attitude in this matter is striking. We would not be willing to consider it even as *improbable* that a missing lawn-chair had "just ceased to exist." We would not entertain such a suggestion. If anyone proposed it we would be sure he was joking. It is no exaggeration to say that this attitude is part of the foundations of our thinking. I do not want to say that this attitude is *un*reasonable; but rather that it is something that we do not *try* to support with grounds. It could be said to belong to "the framework" of our thinking about material things.

Wittgenstein asks: "Does anyone ever test whether this table remains in existence when no one is paying attention to it?" (*OC*, 163). The answer is: Of course not. Is this because we would not call it "a table" if that were to happen? But we do call it "a table" and none of us makes the test. Doesn't this show that we do not regard that occurrence as a possibility? People who did so regard it would seem ludicrous to us. One could imagine that they made ingenious experiments to decide the question; but this research would make us smile. Is this because experiments were conducted by our ancestors that settled the matter once and for all? I don't

believe it. The principle that material things do not cease to exist
without physical cause is an unreflective part of the framework
within which physical investigations are made and physical explanations arrived at.

Wittgenstein suggests that the same is true of what might be
called "the principle of the continuity of nature":

Think of chemical investigations. Lavoisier makes experiments with substances in his laboratory and now concludes that this and that takes place
when there is burning. He does not say that it might happen otherwise
another time. He has got hold of a world-picture—not of course one that
he invented: he learned it as a child. I say world-picture and not hypothesis, because it is the matter-of-course (*selbstverständliche*) foundation for his
research and as such also goes unmentioned (*OC*, 167).

But now, what part is played by the presupposition that a substance A
always reacts to a substance B in the same way, given the same circumstances? Or is that part of the definition of a substance? (*OC*, 168).

Framework principles such as the continuity of nature or the assumption that material things do not cease to exist without physical
cause, belong to what Wittgenstein calls a "system." He makes the
following observation, which seems to me to be true: "All testing,
all confirmation and disconfirmation of a hypothesis takes place already within a system. And this system is not a more or less arbitrary and doubtful point of departure for all our arguments; no, it
belongs to the nature of what we call an argument. The system is
not so much the point of departure, as the element in which arguments have their life" (*OC*, 105).

A "system" provides the boundaries within which we ask questions, carry out investigations, and make judgments. Hypotheses
are put forth, and challenged, *within* a system. Verification, justification, the search for evidence, occur *within* a system. The
framework propositions of the system are not put to the test, not
backed up by evidence. This is what Wittgenstein means when he
says: "Of course there is justification; but justification comes to an
end" (*OC*, 192); and when he asks: "Doesn't testing come to an

end?" (*OC*, 164); and when he remarks that "whenever we test any-thing we are already presupposing something that is not tested" (*OC*, 163).

That this is so is not to be attributed to human weakness. It is a conceptual requirement that our inquiries and proofs stay within boundaries. Think, for example, of the activity of calculating a number. Some steps in a calculation we will check for correctness, but others we won't: for example, that $4 + 4 = 8$. More accurately, some beginners might check it, but grown-ups won't. Similarly, some grown-ups would want to determine by calculation whether $25 \times 25 = 625$, whereas others would regard that as laughable. Thus the boundaries of the system within which *you* calculate may not be exactly the same as my boundaries. But we do calculate; and, as Wittgenstein remarks, "In certain circumstances . . . we regard a calculation as sufficiently checked. What gives us a right to do so? . . . Somewhere we must be finished with justification, and then there remains the proposition that *this* is how we calculate" (*OC*, 212). If someone did not accept any boundaries for calculating, this would mean that he had not learned *that* language-game: "If some-one supposed that *all* our calculations were uncertain and that we could rely on none of them (justifying himself by saying that mis-takes are always possible) perhaps we would say he was crazy. But can we say he is in error? Does he not just react differently? We rely on calculations, he doesn't; we are sure, he isn't" (*OC*, 217). We are taught, or we absorb, the systems within which we raise doubts, make inquiries, draw conclusions. We grow into a frame-work. We don't question it. We accept it trustingly. But this accep-tance is not a consequence of reflection. We do not *decide* to accept framework propositions. We do not decide that we live on the earth, any more than we decide to learn our native tongue. We do come to adhere to a framework proposition, in the sense that it shapes the way we think. The framework propositions that we ac-cept, grow into, are not idiosyncrasies but common ways of speak-ing and thinking that are pressed on us by our human community. For our acceptances to have been withheld would have meant that we had not learned how to count, to measure, to use names, to play games, or even *to talk*. Wittgenstein remarks that "a language-game is only possible if one trusts something." Not *can*, but *does* trust something (OC, 509). I think he means by this trust or acceptance what he calls belief "in the sense of religious belief" (*OC*, 459). What does he mean by belief "in the sense of religious belief"? He explicitly distinguishes it from *conjecture* (*Vermutung:* ibid). I think this means that there is nothing tentative about it; it is not adopted as an hypothesis that might later be withdrawn in the light of new evidence. This also makes explicit an important feature of Wittgenstein's understanding of belief, in the sense of "religious belief," namely, that it does not rise or fall on the basis of evidence or grounds: it is "groundless."

II

In our Western academic philosophy, religious belief is commonly regarded as unreasonable and is viewed with condescension or even contempt. It is said that religion is a refuge for those who, because of weakness of intellect or character, are unable to confront the stern realities of the world. The objective, mature, *strong* attitude is to hold beliefs solely on the basis of *evidence*.

It appears to me that philosophical thinking is greatly influenced by this veneration of evidence. We have an aversion to statements, reports, declarations, beliefs, that are not based on grounds. There are many illustrations of this philosophical bent.

For example, in regard to a person's report that he has an image of the Eiffel Tower we have an inclination to think that the image must *resemble* the Eiffel Tower. How else could the person declare so confidently what his image is *of*? *How could he know*?

Another example: a memory-report or memory-belief must be based, we think, on some mental *datum* that is equipped with various features to match the corresponding features of the memory-belief. This datum will include an image that provides the *content* of the belief, and a peculiar feeling that makes one refer the image to a *past* happening, and another feeling that makes one believe that the image is an *accurate* portrayal of the past happening, and still another feeling that informs one that it was *oneself* who witnessed the past happening. The presence of these various features makes memory-beliefs thoroughly reasonable.

Another illustration: if interrupted in speaking one can usually give a confident account, later on, of what one had been *about* to say. How is this possible? Must not one remember *a feeling of tendency to say just those words?* This is one's basis for knowing what one had been about to say. It justifies one's subsequent account.

Still another example: after dining at a friend's house you announce your intention to go home. How do you know your intention? One theory proposes that you are presently aware of a particular mental state or bodily feeling which, as you recall from your past experience, has been highly correlated with the behavior of going home; so you infer that *that* is what you are going to do now. A second theory holds that you must be aware of some definite mental state or event which reveals itself, not by experience but *intrinsically*, as the intention to go home. Your awareness of that mental item *informs* you of what action you will take.

Yet another illustration: this is the instructive case of the man who, since birth, has been immune to sensations of bodily pain. On his thirtieth birthday he is kicked on the shins, and for the first time he responds by crying out, hopping around on one foot, holding his leg, and exclaiming "The pain is terrible!" We have an overwhelming inclination to wonder, "How could he tell, *this first time*, that what he felt was *pain?*" Of course the implication is that *after* the first time there would be *no* problem. Why not? Because his first experience of pain would provide him with a sample that would be preserved in memory; thereafter he would be equipped to determine whether any sensation he feels is or isn't pain; he would just compare it with the memory-sample to see whether the two match! Thus he will have a *justification* for believing that what he feels is pain. But the *first time* he will not have this justification. This is why the case is so puzzling. Could it be that this first time he *infers* that he is in pain from his own behavior?

A final illustration: consider the fact that after a comparatively few examples and bits of instruction a person can go on to carry out a task, apply a word correctly in the future, continue a numerical series from an initial segment, distinguish grammatical from ungrammatical constructions, solve arithmetical problems, and so on. These correct performances will be dealing with new and different examples, situations, combinations. The performance output will be far more varied than the instruction input. How is this possible? What carries the person from the meager instruction to his rich performance? The explanation has to be that an effect of his training was that he abstracted the Idea, perceived the Common Nature, "internalized" the Rule, grasped the Structure. What else could bridge the gap between the poverty of instruction and the wealth of performance? Thus we postulate an intervening mental act or state which removes the inequality and restores the balance.

My illustrations belong to what could be called the *pathology* of philosophy. Wittgenstein speaks of a "general disease of thinking" which attempts to explain occurrences of discernment, recognition, or understanding, by postulating mental states or proscesses from which those occurrences flow "as from a reservoir" (*BB*, p. 143). These mental intermediaries are assumed to contribute to the causation of the various cognitive performances. More significantly for my present purpose, they are supposed to *justify* them; they provide our *grounds* for saying or doing this rather than that; they *explain how we know*. The Image, or Cognitive State, or Feeling, or Idea, or Sample, or Rule, or Structure, *tells* us. It is like a road map or a signpost. It guides our course.

What is "pathological" about these explanatory constructions and pseudo-scientific inferences? Two things at least. First, the movement of thought that demands these intermediaries is circular and empty, unless it provides criteria for determining their presence and nature *other than* the occurrence of the phenomena they are postulated to explain—and of course no such criteria are forthcoming. Second, there is the great criticism by Wittgenstein of this movement of philosophical thought: namely, his point that no matter what kind of state, process, paradigm, sample, structure, or rule is conceived of as giving us the necessary guidance, *it* could be taken, or understood, as indicating a *different* direction from the one in which we actually did go. The assumed intermediary Idea, Structure, or Rule does not and cannot reveal that because of it we went in the only direction it was reasonable to go. Thus the internalized intermediary we are tempted to invoke to bridge the gap between training and performance, as being that which shows us what we must do or say if we are to be rational, cannot do the job it was invented to do. It cannot fill the epistemological gap. It cannot provide the bridge of justification. It cannot put to rest the How-do-we-know? question. Why not? Because it cannot tell us how *it itself* is to be taken, understood, applied. Wittgenstein puts the point briefly and powerfully: "Don't always think that you read off your words from facts; that you portray these in words according to rules. For even so you would have to apply the rule in the particular case without guidance" (*PI*, 292). Without guidance! Like Wittgenstein's signpost arrow that cannot tell us whether to go in the direction of the arrow tip or in the opposite direction, so too the Images, Ideas, Cognitive Structures, or Rules that we philosophers imagine as devices for guidance cannot interpret themselves to us. The signpost does not tell the traveler how to read it. A second signpost might tell him how to read the first one; we can imagine such a case. But this can't go on. If the traveler is to continue his journey he will have to do something on his own, without guidance.

The parable of the traveler speaks for *all* of the language-games we learn and practice, even those in which there is the most disciplined instruction and the most rigorous standards of conformity. Suppose that a pupil has been given thorough training in some procedure, whether it is drawing patterns, building fences, or proving theorems. But then he has to carry on by himself in new situations. How does he know what to do? Wittgenstein presents the following dialogue: " 'However you instruct him in the continuation of a pattern—how can he *know* how he is to continue by himself?'—Well, how do *I* know?—If that means 'Have I grounds?', the answer is: the grounds will soon give out. And then I shall act, without grounds" (*PI*, 211). Grounds come to an end. Answers to How-do-we-know? questions come to an end. Evidence comes to an end. We must speak, act, live, without evidence. This is so not just on the fringes of life and language, but at the center of our most regularized activities. We do learn rules and learn to follow them. But our training was in the past! We had to leave it behind and proceed on our own.

It is an immensely important fact of nature that as people carry on an activity in which they have received a common training, they do largely *agree* with one another, accepting the same examples and analogies, taking the same steps. We agree in what to say, in how to apply language. We agree in our responses to particular cases.

As Wittgenstein says, "That is not agreement in opinions but in form of life" (*PI*, 241). We cannot explain this agreement by saying that we are just doing what the rules tell us—for our agreement in applying rules, formulae and signposts is what gives them their *meaning*.

One of the primary pathologies of philosophy is the feeling that we must *justify* our language-games. We want to establish them as well grounded. But we should consider here Wittgenstein's remark that a language-game "is not based on grounds. It is there—like our life" (*OC*, 559).

Within a language-game there is justification and lack of justification, evidence and proof, mistakes and groundless opinions, good and bad reasoning, correct measurements and incorrect ones. One cannot properly apply these terms to a language-game itself. It may, however, be said to be "groundless," not in the sense of a groundless opinion, but in the sense that we accept it, we live it. We can say, "This is what we do. This is how we are."

In this sense religion is groundless; and so is chemistry. Within each of these two systems of thought and action there is controversy and argument. Within each there are advances and recessions of insight into the secrets of nature or the spiritual condition of humankind and the demands of the Creator, Savior, Judge, Source. Within the framework of each system there is criticism, explanation, justification. But we should not expect that there might be some sort of rational justification of the framework itself.

A chemist will sometimes employ induction. Does he have evidence for a Law of Induction? Wittgenstein observes that it would strike him as nonsense to say, "I know that the Law of Induction is true." ("Imagine such a statement made in a law court.") It would be more correct to say, "I believe in the Law of Induction" (*OC*, 500). This way of putting it is better because it shows that the attitude toward induction is belief in the sense of "religious" belief— that is to say, an acceptance which is not conjecture or surmise and for which there is no reason—it is a groundless acceptance.

It is intellectually troubling for us to conceive that a whole system of thought might be groundless, might have no rational justification. We realize easily enough, however, that grounds soon give out—that we cannot go on giving reasons for our reasons. There arises from this realization the conception of a reason that is *self-justifying*—something whose credentials as a reason cannot be questioned.

This metaphysical conception makes its presence felt at many points—for example, as an explanation of how a person can tell what his mental image is *of*. We feel that the following remarks, imagined by Wittgenstein, are exactly right: " 'The image must be more similar to its object than any picture. For however similar I make the picture to what it is supposed to represent, it can always be the picture of something else. But it is essential to the image that it is the image of *this* and of nothing else' " (*PI*, 389). A pen and ink drawing represents the Eiffel Tower; but it could represent a mine shaft or a new type of automobile jack. Nothing prevents this drawing from being taken as a representation of something other than the Eiffel Tower. But my mental image of the Eiffel Tower is *necessarily* an image of the Eiffel Tower. Therefore it must be a "remarkable" kind of picture. As Wittgenstein observes: "Thus one might come to regard the image as a super-picture" (ibid.). Yet we have no intelligible conception of how a super-picture would differ from an ordinary picture. It would seem that it has to be a *super-likeness*—but what does this mean?

There is a familiar linguistic practice in which one person *tells* another what his image is of (or what he intends to do, or what he was about to say) and no question is raised of how the first one *knows* that what he says is true. This question is imposed from outside, artificially, by the philosophical craving for justification. We can see here the significance of these remarks: "It isn't a question of explaining a language-game by means of our experiences, but of noting a language-game" (*PI*, 665). "Look on the language-game as the *primary* thing" (*PI*, 656). Within a system of thinking and acting there occurs, *up to a point*, investigation and criticism of the reasons and justifications that are employed in that system. This inquiry into whether a reason is good or adequate cannot, as said, go on endlessly. We stop it. We bring it to an end. We come upon something that *satisfies* us. It is *as if* we made a decision or issued an edict: "*This* is an adequate reason!" (or explanation, or justification). Thereby we fix a boundary of our language-game.

There is nothing wrong with this. How else could we have disciplines, systems, games? But our fear of groundlessness makes us conceive that we are under some logical compulsion to terminate at *those particular* stopping points. We imagine that we have confronted the self-evident reason, the self-justifying explanation, the picture or symbol whose meaning cannot be questioned. This obscures from us the *human* aspect of our concepts—the fact that what we call "a reason," "evidence," "explanation," "justification," is what appeals to and satisfies *us*.

III

The desire to provide a rational foundation for a form of life is especially prominent in the philosophy of religion, where there is an intense preoccupation with purported proofs of the existence of God. In American universities there must be hundreds of courses in which these proofs are the main topic. We can be sure that nearly always the critical verdict is that the proofs are invalid and consequently that, up to the present time at least, religious belief has received no rational justification.

Well, of course not! The obsessive concern with the proofs reveals the assumption that in order for religious belief to be intellectually respectable it *ought* to have a rational justification. *That* is the misunderstanding. It is like the idea that we are not justified in relying on memory until memory has been proved reliable.

Roger Trigg makes the following remark: "To say that someone acts in a certain way because of his belief in God does seem to be more than a redescription of his action. . . . It is to give a reason for it. The belief is distinct from the commitment which may follow it, and is the justification for it." [2] It is evident from other remarks that by "belief in God" Trigg means "belief in the existence of God" or "belief that God exists." Presumably by the *acts* and *commitments* of a religious person Trigg refers to such things as prayer, worship, confession, thanksgiving, partaking of sacraments, and participation in the life of a religious group.

For myself I have great difficulty with the notion of belief in *the existence* of God, whereas the idea of belief *in* God is to me intelligible. If a man did not ever pray for help or forgiveness, or have any inclination toward it; nor ever felt that it is "a good and joyful thing" to thank God for the blessings of this life; nor was ever concerned about his failure to comply with divine commandments—then, it seems clear to me, he could not be said to believe in God. Belief in God is not an all or none thing; it can be more or less; it can wax and wane. But belief in God in any degree does require, as I understand the words, some religious action, some commitment, or if not, at least a bad conscience.

According to Trigg, if I take him correctly, a man who was entirely devoid of any inclination to religious action or conscience might believe in *the existence* of God. What would be the marks of this? Would it be that the man knows some theology, can recite the

2. Trigg, *Reason and Commitment* (Cambridge, 1973), p. 75.

Creeds, is well-read in Scripture? Or is his belief in the existence of God something different from this? If so, what? What would be the difference between a man who knows some articles of faith, heresies, Scriptural writings, and in addition believes in the existence of God, and one who knows these things but does not believe in the existence of God? I assume that both of them are indifferent to the acts and commitments of religious life.

I do not comprehend this notion of belief in *the existence* of God which is thought to be distinct from belief *in* God. It seems to me to be an artificial construction of philosophy, another illustration of the craving for justification.

Religion is a form of life; it is language embedded in action—what Wittgenstein calls a "language-game." Science is another. Neither stands in need of justification, the one no more than the other.

Present-day academic philosophers are far more prone to challenge the credentials of religion than of science. This is probably due to a number of things. One may be the illusion that science can justify its own framework. Another is the fact that science is a vastly greater force in our culture. Still another reason may be the fact that by and large religion is to university people an alien form of life. They do not participate in it and do not understand what it is all about. This non-understanding is of an interesting nature. It derives, at least in part, from the inclination of academics to suppose that their employment as scholars demands of them the most severe objectivity and dispassionateness. For an academic philosopher to become a religious believer would be a stain on his professional competence! Here I will quote from Nietzsche, who was commenting on the relation of the German scholar of his day to religious belief; yet his remarks continue to have a nice appropriateness for the American and British scholars of our own day:

Pious or even merely church-going people seldom realize *how much* good will, one might even say willfulness, it requires nowadays for a German scholar to take the problem of religion seriously; his whole trade . . . disposes him to a superior, almost good-natured merriment in regard to

religion, sometimes mixed with a mild contempt directed at the 'unclean-
liness' of spirit which he presupposes wherever one still belongs to the
church. It is only with the aid of history (thus *not* from his personal experience) that the scholar succeeds in summoning up a reverent seriousness
and a certain shy respect towards religion; but if he intensifies his feelings
towards it even to the point of feeling grateful to it, he has still in his own
person not got so much as a single step closer to that which still exists as
church or piety; perhaps the reverse. The practical indifference to religious
things in which he was born and raised is as a rule sublimated in him into
a caution and cleanliness which avoids contact with religious people and
things; . . . Every age has its own divine kind of naïvety for the invention
of which other ages may envy it—and how much naïvety, venerable,
childlike and boundlessly stupid naïvety there is in the scholar's belief in
his superiority, in the good conscience of his tolerance, in the simple un-
suspecting certainty with which his instinct treats the religious man as an
inferior and lower type which he himself has grown beyond and *above*. [3]

IV

Someone could point out that within particular religions there
are beliefs that are based on evidence or to which evidence is relevant. This is indeed so. Some doctrinal beliefs about Jesus and the
Holy Spirit, for example, are based on New Testament texts. Here
is an area where evidence and interpretation are appropriate. There
are disputes between Christian sects (for example, the controversy
over the authority of the Bishop of Rome)—disputes to which tex-
tual evidences are relevant.

In the present essay I have been talking not about this or that
doctrinal belief but, more generally, about *religious belief*. It would
be convenient if I could substitute the words "belief in God" for
the words "religious belief"; but I hesitate to do so because the
Buddhists, for example, do not describe themselves as believing in
God, and yet Buddhism is undoubtedly a religion. Religious belief
as such, not particular creeds or doctrines, is my topic.

I think there can be evidence for the particular doctrines of a
faith only within the attitude of religious belief. Many people who

3. Nietzsche, *Beyond Good and Evil*, trans. R. J. Hollingdale (Penguin Classics),
para. 58.

read about incidents in the life of Jesus, as recounted in the Gospels, or about events in the lives of the Hebrew prophets, as recounted in the Old Testament, do not believe that the reported incidents actually occurred. But it is possible to believe that they occurred without regarding them as *religiously significant*. That a man should die and then come to life again is not necessarily of religious significance. That the apparent motion of the sun should be interrupted, as related in Joshua, does not have to be understood religiously. A well-known physicist once remarked to me, only *half*-humorously, that a study of the causation of miracles could be a branch of applied physics! Biblical miracles *can* be regarded as events of merely scientific interest. They can be viewed from either a scientific or a religious *Weltanschauung*. It is only from the viewpoint of religious belief that they have religious import.

It is such a viewpoint or *Weltbild* (to use Wittgenstein's term), whether religious or scientific, that I am holding to be "groundless." I am not saying, of course, that these different ways of picturing the world do not have *causes*. Education, culture, family upbringing, can foster a way of seeing the world. A personal disaster can destroy, or produce, religious belief. Religious people often think of their own belief as a result of God's intervention in their lives.

My interest, however, is not in causes. What I am holding is that a religious viewpoint is not based on grounds or evidence, whether this is the Five Ways of Aquinas, the starry heavens, or whatever. Of course, some people do *see* the wonders of nature as *manifestations* of God's loving presence. Someone might even be able to regard the Five Ways in that light. Anselm did thank God for His gift of the Ontological Proof. But seeing something as a manifestation of God's love or creative power is a very different thing from taking it either as evidence for an empirical hypothesis or as a kind of logical proof of the correctness of religious belief.

Some readers may want to know whether my position is that people do not *in fact* seek grounds for their religious belief, or whether, as a conceptual matter, there *could not* be grounds. I hold that both things are true, even though this may shock a well-trained analytic philosopher. When you are describing a language-game, a system of thought and action, you are describing concepts, and yet also describing what certain people do—how they think, react, live. Wittgenstein reminds us that in doing mathematical calculations we do not worry about the figures changing shape after being written down; and also that scientists usually are not in doubt as to whether they are in their laboratories. That such doubts are rare is an empirical fact; yet if it were not for this kind of fact we *could not* have some of our concepts. Consider these remarks by Wittgenstein:

Mathematicians do not in general quarrel over the result of a calculation. (This is an important fact.)—If it were otherwise, if for instance, one mathematician was convinced that a figure had altered unperceived, or that memory had deceived either him or the other person, and so on—then our concept of "mathematical certainty" would not exist" (*PI*, p. 225).

If I am trying to mate someone in chess, I cannot be having doubts as to whether the pieces are perhaps changing positions of themselves and at the same time my memory is tricking me so that I don't notice it (*OC*, 346).

I know that some philosophers would like to have a *demonstration* that religious belief is groundless. I do not know what "demonstration" could mean here. But I will say this: it is obvious that the wonders and horrors of nature, the history of nations, great events in personal experience, music, art, the Ontological Proof, and so on—can be responded to either religiously or nonreligiously. Suppose there is a person who is untouched by any inclination toward religious belief, and another who wants to present him convincing grounds for religious belief. Can he do it? I don't see how. The first person can regard the presented "evidence" as psychologically, historically, mythologically, or logically interesting—perhaps fascinating. But even if he has an "open mind," the proffered phenomena or reasoning cannot have religious import for him unless he has at least an inclination toward a religious *Weltbild*. This is the necessary medium, the atmosphere, within which these "evidences" can have religious significance. Wittgenstein's remarks about "the language-game," namely that

> It is not based on grounds.
> It is not reasonable (or unreasonable).
> It is there—like our life (*OC*, 599)

are meant to apply to all language-games, but seem to be true in an especially obvious way of religious belief.

Belief in a God who creates, judges, and loves humanity is *one form* of religious belief. Belief in a mystical principle of causality according to which good produces good and evil produces evil is *another form* of religious belief. Those perspectives on reality are not hypotheses for or against which evidence can be marshalled. You may invite someone to see the world as a heartless mechanism or, on the contrary, as throbbing with love. Once a person has the beginnings of such a vision you may strengthen it for him by means of luminous examples. But unless he already shares that vision in some degree, he will not take your examples in the way you want him to take them. It may be that your conviction, passion, love, will move him in the direction of religious belief. But this would be speaking of causes, not grounds.

Index

Thought and Knowledge

Designed by R. E. Rosenbaum.
Composed by Vail-Ballou Press, Inc.,
in 10 point VIP Janson, 3 points leaded,
with display lines in Janson.
Printed offset by Vail-Ballou Press
Warren's No. 66 text, 50 pound basis.
Bound by Vail-Ballou Press
in Joanna book cloth
and stamped in All Purpose foil.

Library of Congress Cataloging in Publication Data
(For library cataloging purposes only)

Malcolm, Norman, 1911–
    Thought and knowledge.

    Includes bibliographical references.
    CONTENTS: Descartes' proof that his essence is thinking.—
Thoughtless brutes.—Descartes' proof that he is essentially a non-material
thing.—Behaviorism as a philosophy of psychology. [etc.]
    Includes index.
    1. Knowledge, Theory of—Addresses, essays, lectures.   I. Title.
BD161.M283   121   76-25647
ISBN 0-8014-1074-6